Governor Zell Miller's Reading Initiative

100
ATHLETES
WHO SHAPED SPORTS HISTORY

Timothy Jacobs

with

Mark Raymond Aston

Assistant to the Sports Editor
San Francisco Chronicle

A Bluewood Book

This edition produced and published in 1994 by Bluewood Books
A Division of The Siyeh Group, Inc.,
P.O. Box 460313
San Francisco, CA 94146

ISBN 0-912517-13-1

Printed in USA

Designed by Tom Debolski
and Ruth DeJauregui
Edited by Bill Yenne

Illustrations by Vadim Vahrameev

Key to front cover illustration:
1. Babe Didrikson Zaharias
2. Jim Thorpe
3. Pele
4. Paavo Nurmi
5. Sonja Henie
6. Ancient Greek Athlete
7. Babe Ruth
8. Wilt Chamberlain

About the Author:
Timothy Jacobs is the author and editor of numerous volumes including *The Golf Courses of Robert Trent Jones Jr, The Golf Courses of Jack Nicklaus,* and *Great Golf Courses of the World.* Mr. Jacobs currently resides in Northern California with his wife and two children.

TABLE OF CONTENTS

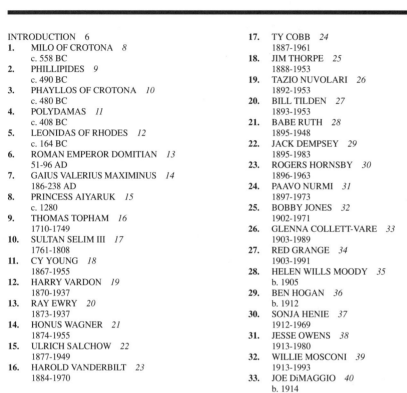

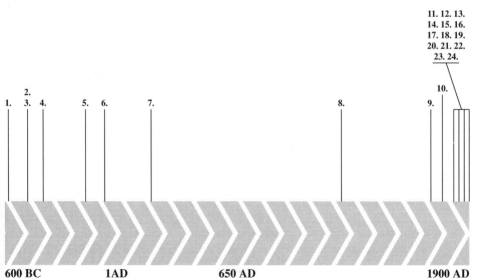

600 BC   1AD   650 AD   1900 AD

34.	BABE DIDRIKSON ZAHARIAS *41*	
	1914-1956	
35.	JOE LOUIS *42*	
	1914-1981	
36.	MARION LADEWIG *43*	
	b. 1914	
37.	PATTY BERG *44*	
	b. 1918	
38.	TED WILLIAMS *45*	
	b. 1918	
39.	JACKIE ROBINSON *46*	
	1919-1972	
40.	JOHN DAVIS *47*	
	1921-1984	
41.	ROCKY MARCIANO *48*	
	1923-1969	
42.	GEORGE MIKAN *49*	
	b. 1924	
43.	DON CARTER *50*	
	b. 1926	
44.	BOB COUSY *51*	
	b. 1928	
45.	GORDIE HOWE *52*	
	b. 1928	
46.	ARNOLD PALMER *53*	
	b. 1929	
47.	JACQUES PLANTE *54*	
	1929-1986	
48.	ROGER BANNISTER *55*	
	b. 1929	
49.	PAT McCORMICK *56*	
	b. 1930	
50.	BILL SHOEMAKER *57*	
	b. 1931	

51.	BILL RUSSELL *58*	
	b. 1934	
52.	HENRY AARON *59*	
	b. 1934	
53.	LARYSSA LATYNINA *60*	
	b. 1934	
54.	A.J. FOYT *61*	
	b. 1935	
55.	SANDY KOUFAX *62*	
	b. 1935	
56.	WILT CHAMBERLAIN *63*	
	b. 1936	
57.	JIM BROWN *64*	
	b. 1936	
58.	RICHARD PETTY *65*	
	b. 1937	
59.	ROD LAVER *66*	
	b. 1938	
60.	JACK NICKLAUS *67*	
	b. 1940	
61.	MARIO ANDRETTI *68*	
	b. 1940	
62.	PELE *69*	
	b. 1940	
63.	MARGARET SMITH COURT *70*	
	b. 1942	
64.	MUHAMMAD ALI *71*	
	b. 1942	
65.	VASILI ALEXEYEV *72*	
	b. 1942	
66.	PHIL ESPOSITO *73*	
	b. 1942	
67.	LARRY MAHAN *74*	
	b. 1943	

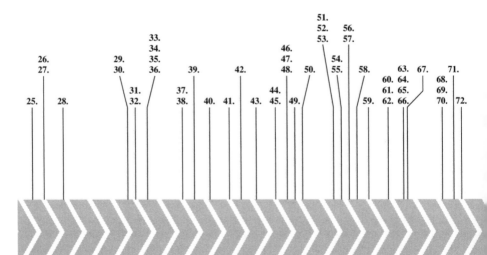

1900 AD   1925   1950

4

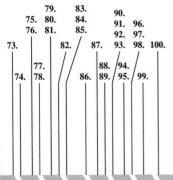

1950   1975   2000

INTRODUCTION

Sports are an integral part of our history. On one hand, serving as a barometer of human progress, and on the other, a measure of human aspiration, organized sporting activity has tended to flourish when civilizations have reached their zenith. Nations take pride in their athletes, who represent the vigor of their cultures.

Citizens of the twentieth century world enjoy an unparalleled interest in — and opportunities for — sports and athletics. Only ancient Greece and Rome had developed the concept of games as international events as extensively as we have in our time.

While not many strong men carry heifers on their shoulders these days, it was considered a newsworthy event when the formidable multi-athlete **Milo of Crotona** did it. Milo's is the only story from that legendary time, when athletes were sponsored by — and sometimes were — emperors, as was the giant Roman Emperor **Maximius**.

This was a concept that would rise sharply in the Middle Ages, when the far-reaching aegis of empire gave way to feudal states, placing a premium on skill at arms. Empire has always been an aid to chroniclers of human events. When empires gave way to feudal states, the Church was the only curator of what had gone before, and even monastic archives were not sufficient to save much of our ancient heritage.

We do know that running, jumping and such as the shot put ("putting the stone") continued in currency, but not many records of such contests, *if kept,* are now extant. Even so, a strikingly contemporary note peals forth in the example of the unbeatable wrestler, Tartar Princess **Aiyaruk**.

As feudal states were united into larger, national units, usually in the interest of some larger cause, the Crusades, perhaps, or regaining long-lost land rights, the populace had marginally more time to play, and chroniclers were given to write about this growing sense of leisure.

In the vanguard of sports mentioned in the early Renaissance was a game played with sticks and a ball, that evolved into our modern game of golf, which would be brought to perfection by the likes of **Harry Vardon, Jack Nicklaus** and **Babe Didrikson Zaharias**. Various other games played with various sizes and shapes of balls would be developed into our modern day soccer, football, handball and the myriad of other ball games we play today. Even if we have no specific names for the heroes of those days, we have an image of the game, especially as played by **Ted Williams,**

Michael Jordan and **Martina Navratilova**.

And of course, that's what fans want — an image of the game that magically supplants the image of themselves with that of a famous sports figure, whose name everyone knows.

Our present world is a heady mix of a wealth of material goods that has not been seen, perhaps since the days of ancient Rome. Added to this is our industry-oriented competitive spirit. The machines of the Industrial Revolution increased everything: the pace of work, the intensity of competition, and the amount of goods that could be gained by outpacing one's fellow humans. Technology has added to that, and has added to sports performance notably.

But even more than that, men and women like **Jim Thorpe, Jackie Joyner-Kersee, Henry Aaron, Joe Montana, Chris Evert** and others have proven that it is the indomitable human spirit, the desire to excel, that has driven athletes from ancient Greece to modern Michigan to excel — hoping for more than to "break the record," hoping to touch the ultimate boundary of their own ability.

This book proposes a list of 100 athletes whose achievements have moved the sense of competition up a notch or two — and have, with their own personal talent, striving and unique sense of discipline, changed the history of sports.

1. MILO OF CROTONA
c. 558 BC (Wrestler, Weightlifter)

Born in Crotona (a region now known as Calabria) in 558 BC, **Milo** was as large in life as most Greek heroes were in myth. His athletic career, which coincided with the era of the original Olympic Games, spanned 25 years, and brought him much notoriety. He may have been the *most dominant* athlete in any sport of all time. As an ancient writer put it: "Neither god nor man could stand against him!"

The image of Milo left us by antiquity is that of a man carrying a four-year-old heifer on his shoulders. The weight thus carried is estimated as at least 900 pounds, and the records are clear: Milo carried the heifer *on his shoulders*, thus presenting a highly difficult lifting feat. This is combined with the distance carried — the length of the Olympian stadium, which was in excess of 600 feet (600 ancient Olympic feet equals 630.74 modern US feet).

Milo was the wrestling champion in six Olympian, seven Pythian, nine Nemean and 10 Isthmian Games. He failed to win his seventh Olympics only because — and here we have two divergent accounts — either wrestling was cancelled because none of his competitors had the courage to show up for the competition; or, his lone competitor, Timastheos, refused to come near him, once in the wrestling arena.

Milo was considered to be the greatest of all ancient Olympian athletes. As was sometimes the practice with highly-revered athletes, a huge bronze statue was created in his honor. The statue was a problem, however — it had to be transported to the Altis ("high place") at Olympia, and no one could engineer a way to do it. Rather than suffer this setback to his honor, Milo cooperatively picked the statue up, carried it to the Altis, and placed it there.

Fragments of Greek writings are the source of all we know about Milo: when he died, how he died, we are not sure — but the record stands clear that he was truly a phenomenon of the ancient athletic world.

Milo of Crotona

2. PHILLIPIDES
c. 490 BC (Runner)

Phillipides was an Athenian Greek. He was a trained athletic runner and messenger who set a rare example of dedication, courage and stamina. He also unwittingly established what is now known as a "marathon" when he ran 26 miles nonstop, from the Greek city of Marathon to Athens, to bring news of the Greek victory over the Persians in the Battle of Marathon.

As a runner, Phillipides had actually made his mark in the ancient world just shortly before making the Marathon run. This was when he finished a run from Athens to Sparta, a distance of 158 miles, to call for reinforcements. He covered the distance in one day, according to Herodotus, who recorded the event in 430 BC.

He then *immediately returned* from Sparta to Athens, for a total round trip of *315 miles in two and one-half days of running*, and then polished it off with his famous 26-mile run to announce the victory. These accomplishments are doubly amazing when you consider that the Greek athlete's choice of footwear was either *barefoot* or *sandals*.

While Plutarch, writing in 100 AD, maintains that a soldier named Eukles actually made the Marathon run, his statement that the soldier ran the distance while still clad in his bronze armor, after the heat of battle, makes this claim doubtful.

Since all authors writing of the event relied on either oral or transcribed eye-witness accounts, we tend to believe the earlier account of Herodotus, since it was written much closer in time to the actual event. Upon his arrival in Athens after his all-out 26-mile run, Phillipides is said to have cried, "Be happy! We have won!" and died of exhaustion on the spot. His stamina and courage are now evoked whenever a runner of extraordinary marathon ability emerges.

Phillipides set an inspired example for all runners to follow. That he established one of the great racing distances, and that it remains in use even today, is an "endurance record" (of another kind) of *2484 years*!

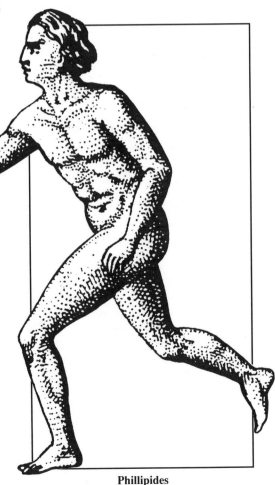

Phillipides

3. PHAYLLOS OF CROTONA
c. 480 BC (Pentathlete)

In the ancient world, the Pentathlon was a competitive sporting event composed of the long jump, discus throw, wrestling, 200-yard dash, and javelin throw, though not necessarily in that order. **Phayllos** was the most famous of all Greek Pentathletes.

He performed his deeds within a century after Milo of Crotona had amazed the ancient world with his legendary career. Phayllos won the Pentathlon at the Pythian Games at Delphi twice, and was also a champion runner in events apart from the Pentathlon.

One of Phayllos' deeds even became a slang term along the lines of our contemporary "pushing the envelope." In Phayllos' case, the lingo was "beyond the dug-up area," in reference to a record-breaking long jump he had made: 55 feet, or five feet beyond the landing pit.

It should be understood that the "feet" we are using in these records are Delphic feet, which were roughly seven inches long (by contrast, a "foot" at Olympia was more than 12 and one-half inches). This makes Phayllos' broad jump approximately 33 of our feet. Also take into account that Greek long jumpers used four-pound weights in each hand to add momentum to their jumps, though the take-off run was a comparatively short one, and may have offset the advantage of using weights.

Another of Phayllos' famous marks in competition was a 95-foot discus throw. It is almost impossible to make comparisons with current discus records, as the discus in Phayllos' day was made of stone, and ranged in weight from 2.75 pounds to 12.5 pounds, and sizes varied accordingly.

One has to assume that the ancients took these variances into account when establishing championships. The Greek style of discus throwing also involved only one

Phayllos of Crotona

step forward, and the discus was thrown in a vertical arc.

We have the authority of such eminent ancient writers — writing *after* Phayllos' time — as Herodotus, Pausanius, Zenobius and Scholion to say that Phayllos was one of the greatest of the ancient athletes.

4. POLYDAMAS
c. 408 BC (Boxer, Wrestler)

The ancient Greek games featured an event called the *Pankration*, which combined boxing and wrestling. Probably the greatest athlete of the ancient world in this event was **Polydamas**. He had won many pankration championships, including one at Olympia in 408 BC, and was legendary for his strength throughout the Mediterranean region.

In fact, Lucian, a chronicler writing circa 2 AD, places Polydamas in a pantheon of great athletes that includes him, Milo of Crotona (**see no. 1**) and Glaukos, an athlete whom the present author has been able to find no knowledge on.

The ancient Greek chronicler Pausanius hailed Polydamas as the largest man in all of Greece, and estimates made from statuary are that he was six feet, eight inches tall and weighed approximately 300 pounds. His strength was known and envied far and wide — it should be remembered that, while nations take pride in their athletes in the present day, in the ancient world, rulers of nations took a highly personal interest in their athletes.

King Darius I of Persia was such a ruler. Jealous of Grecian good fortune in having Polydamas as a champion, he invited Polydamas to his court for a contest against three of his strongest warriors, his personal bodygaurds, so highly skilled in hand-to-hand combat that they were called "the Immortals."

Polydamas is said to have dispatched all three of the Immortals, and lived to continue his exploits. Among those exploits are the following: unarmed, and attacked by a lion, Polydamas is said to have killed the animal with his bare hands; he once grabbed onto a chariot that was already under way, and successfully held the vehicle back, despite the frantic attempts of its two-horse team to get away.

In doing these things, Polydamas was realizing his desire to emulate the deeds of the mythic Greek warrior Herakles — who was his hero.

According to Pausanius, Polydamas died during a cave-in while trying to support the roof of a cave that he and his friends had entered to escape the summer heat.

Polydamas

5. LEONIDAS OF RHODES
c. 164 BC (Runner)

Three of the chief foot races run at the ancient Olympics were the *hoplitodromos,* in which the runners ran while wearing shin guards and helmets, and carried shields; the *stadion,* in which they would run the length of the stadium; and the *diaulos,* in which they ran the length of the stadium and back.

Leonidas of Rhodes won all three races in four successive Olympiads, 164-152 BC — an unprecedented feat that wrought changes in the sports philosophy of his day.

Before he accomplished this feat, much thought was given to the differences between the three races. In fact, the chronicler Philostratos, writing in 230 AD, explains in detail just what kinds of physiques contestants in each of these events would have ideally possessed:

Hoplitodromos runners should have had long waists, well-developed shoulders and knees "tilted upward (sic)," so that they could carry their shields easily.

The stadion required a slender, somewhat tall (but "not too tall") athlete, solidly built, chest a bit smaller than normal, "legs balanced with the shoulders," solidly built, but not too muscular, with strong hands(!?).

Diaulos runners would have best been "stronger than those for the stadion, but lighter than those for the hoplitodromos."

Philostratos cavils a bit when he says "No one any longer makes any distinction between the physiques of the contestants for the hoplitodromos, the stadion and the diaulos ..." (since Leonidas accomplished the feat described above) "... [S]till, we should distinguish between those entering just one of these races and those entering all of them."

It just proves that old habits die hard. Not much else is known about Leonidas of Rhodes, but that he was a superb runner who essentially changed his sport.

Leonidas of Rhodes

Bows and arrows were important parts of the national armory of such ancient nations as Greece and Persia. Rome, on the other hand, viewed archery as one of the enemy's weapons, but not their own, since the Roman *testudo*, or "turtle" — soldiers holding interlocked shields above their heads — was considered an adequate way of dealing with milieus involving attack by archers.

On the other hand, several Roman emperors took up the bow and arrow as a sport, and practiced it seriously. Probably the most important emperor in establishing archery as a pastime was **Domitian**.

His skill was said to be very high. For exhibitions, he would have a servant stand several yards away. The servant then held his hand out away from his body, and stretched his fingers wide. Domitian would then shoot an arrow between each of the servant's fingers, without so much as grazing the servant.

This inspired others to take up the sport, thus firmly establishing archery as a sporting proposition in ancient Rome. Indeed, one of Domitian's "heirs" in archery was Emperor Commodus (161-192 AD), who put on exhibitions in the Roman arena.

Domitian also established Greek Olympic-style games in Rome. While Greek games were held in Roman Greek colonies after Rome came to dominate the Mediterranean region, Domitian established the first regularly held Greek-style athletic contests on Roman soil.

Domitian named the games the Capitoline Games, and they were immediately included in the list of Greek "Sacred Games," and were seen as second only to the Olympics themselves.

The Capitoline Games were quadrennial, and had three main contest divisions. These were music, equestrian and gymnastics, and even included races for the maid-

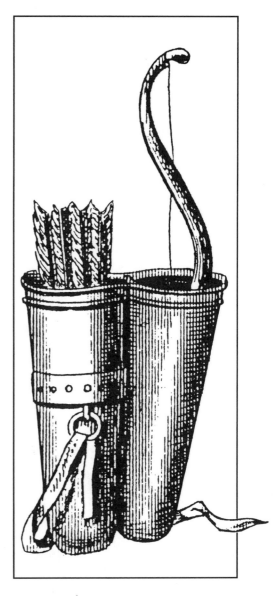

ens (women were generally forbidden in the ancient Greek games). There was also singing, accompaniment and solo-playing for instruments.

Thus, Emperor Domitian made positive advancements in several realms of the sports world of his time.

1. GAIUS VALERIUS MAXIMINUS
186-238 AD (Wrestler, Runner)

Maximinus was a Roman Emperor who ruled from 235 to 238 AD. All that we know of his accomplishments was that he was accounted as the best runner and wrestler of of his time. In his youth, he defeated trained heavyweight wrestlers two and three at a time, "as though they were children, and without getting out of breath," according to athletics expert David Willoughby, in his book *The Super Athletes.*

Maximinus also had tremendous endurance as a runner, and is credited as being the best runner of his time. His hands were huge — this must have helped him in wrestling: legend has it that he could wear his wife's bracelet as a ring!

Maximus was a giant, standing eight feet, one inch tall, and weighing between 400 and 500 pounds. This no doubt aided him in his exploits — which is fairly rare in the history of sports champions, when you consider that size and strength are only two components of a complex athletic formula that also includes stamina, agility, timing and coordination.

Maximinus established one of the few instances in which an outstanding athlete also went on to become the leader of a nation.

Of course, the vagaries of national politics being what they were in Rome, Maximinus, who became emperor in 235 AD, was assassinated just three years later.

Gaius Valerius Maximinus

8. PRINCESS AIYARUK
c. 1280 (Wrestler)

It was a tradition in some ancient countries to make suitors for a princess' hand go through trials by ordeal — perhaps slaying a lion with a spear, or vanquishing a local expert in arms, or at the very least, bringing treasure with them.

Sometimes, though, the trial involved sheer sport. In the Greek myths, there is the story of Atalanta and the Golden Apples, whereby the swift-running maiden defeated her suitors herself by outrunning them.

The following is a story from recorded history, about a princess unlike many others, whose would-be princes had to undergo trial by the strength of *her* arm.

Aiyaruk was a Tartar princess, the daughter of King Kaidu, whose seat of power was at Samarkand in what is now Uzbekistan. Many suitors came to woo Aiyaruk, mainly because of her father's wealth, evidenced by his magnificent palace.

Aiyaruk was a large young woman, modern estimates of her size being perhaps six feet, two inches in height and weighing an estimated 275 pounds. Her suitors had to wrestle her for her hand in marriage.

If they lost, they had to pay her 100 horses. Marco Polo wrote that, by the year 1280, she had obtained a herd of "more than 10,000 horses" this way. That counts for at least 100 matches won, and since she was still unmarried, she had lost none.

This also attests to the fact that these matches were in earnest, horses having been of great value to the Tartar people.

There finally arrived a champion wrestler from Pamir, a neighboring country. He was so confident that he could beat the wrestling princess that he had brought an enormous herd of horses with him, numbering perhaps 1000 horses.

The struggle was intense and prolonged, but the suitor was eventually forced to the

Princess Aiyaruk

mat, and had to forfeit his huge herd of horses. Aiyaruk was perhaps the only woman wrestler ever whose opponents were strictly men, and who was invincible even on those terms.

THOMAS TOPHAM
1710-1749 (Weightlifter, Wrestler)

Student of physical culture David Willoughby theorizes in his book *The Super Athletes*, that some individuals are true prodigies, being naturally endowed to outperform the rest of us. Willoughby's conception of physical prodigies is that they are simply *built* differently than the rest of us — tendons are attached to bone in such as way as to give them superior muscular leverage, their glands secrete just a little more strength-giving substance for them than us, and other physical factors — accounting for strength that is disproportionate to height and weight.

Thomas Topham was a physical prodigy. Five feet, 10 inches tall, 196 pounds in his prime, he wouldn't have struck anyone as unusual — until he spoke. His voice was a deep contrabass: it seemed superhuman. He also had a limp, the result of an injury sustained when the ground gave way as he was restraining two draft horses for an exhibition: the accident shattered one of his kneecaps. This happened when he was 25, at the *beginning* of his phenomenal exhibition career.

He was the son of a carpenter, and though trained in his father's profession, at the age of 25, he became manager of the Red Lion Inn, on City Road, in London.

His feats are numerous and well-attested. He was the strong man on which all strong men to follow have based their routines. He could bend an inch-thick iron poker around a man's neck like a bow tie, and untie it easily. This was proven when one of his customers insulted him, and rather than commit manslaughter, which it surely would have been had a fight ensued, Topham decided to embarrass the man by giving him an iron yoke, which he later removed by unbending the poker.

His finger strength was such that he once cracked a coconut one-handed, in the same manner expert cooks crack eggs. At another exhibition, he carried a full-grown horse over a postern gate. At still another, he lifted a two hundredweight (224 pounds) with his little finger and "lifted it gently over his head;" likewise, he lifted a 27-stone (378-pound) man with only one of his arms.

His most famous feat was a harness lift, while standing on a platform of three heavy casks weighing a total of 1836 pounds, which he performed at a large celebration in honor of the British victory at the Spanish port of Cartagena on April 1, 1741.

All of this was accomplished *after* Topham's leg was crippled, as was his exhibition of wrestling prowess in defeating six trained wrestlers all at once.

Many other astonishing feats are attributed to him, including pranks that only one with his astounding strength could perform: carrying a sleeping sentry *and his sentry box* several blocks to confuse the sentry when he awoke; seizing hold of the rear end of a horsedrawn carriage and pulling it backwards, even as the horse struggled to go forward; and, even with his shattered kneecap, managing to jog for one-half mile while carrying a three hundredweight (336-pound) barrel of nails.

But, as if in proof that physical prowess does not avail against the more delicate issues that life provides, Topham injured himself after storming out of his home following a quarrel with his wife. He died as a result of his injury at the age of 39, on August 10, 1749.

10. SULTAN SELIM III
1761-1808 (Archer)

Sultan Selim was a Turkish ruler whose practice of the sport of archery proved not only his own prowess, but also a Turkish national boast as well.

As we have seen in the case of Roman Emperor **Domitian** (51-96 AD) **(see no. 6)**, archery has sometimes been the sport of emperors and kings. In this tradition, the Turkish court in the eighteenth century took its archery very seriously.

Then again, equipment in any sport tends to improve over the years, catastrophe notwithstanding. That some nations boast of superior athletes is not surprising; and it's no more a surprise when nations boast of superior *equipment*. The Turks held this value dear, as well.

In 1796, a Turkish ambassador visiting England boasted loudly that Turkish bows were better than English bows. The English, whose roots in archery go back to ancient times, proposed he prove his boast.

With that, the ambassador selected a bow from the exhibition case in the Diplomatic Building. It was an old bow, dating back to the era of the Seljuk Turks (1000 - 1300 AD). The ambassador touched an arrow to his bow, pulled it back, and shot it 482 yards — which at the time would have been a long distance with a *modern* bow.

Two years later, in 1798, Sultan Selim III set out to prove Turkish archery prowess once and for all.

When archers shoot for sheer *distance*, they generally use what is called "freestyle shooting."

This means that the archer lies on his back, braces his feet against the bow, and pulls the string back with both hands. This is probably the method Sultan Selim III used.

Unsheathing an arrow and firmly grasping one of his good Turkish bows, he set himself up in the "freestyle," strained the string back and shot the arrow 972 yards and two-and three-quarters inches, setting a distance record that has stood for almost two centuries. By present calculation, this feat would have demanded a bow having a "pull" of 250-plus pounds.

The Sultan set a precedent for personal power and equipment strength that has stimulated development of better and stronger bows to the present time.

Sultan Selim III

He was born on a farm near Gilmore, Ohio, with the name **Denton True Young**. He was to earn his famous nickname, "Cy," when he was 23, while trying out as a pitcher for the Canton team of the Tri-State League in the spring of 1890. He threw the ball so hard against the team's star batter, who didn't hit even so much as a foul, that the grandstand behind the batting box was dented and splintered by the attack. He made the team. One of the bystanders dubbed him "Cyclone," later shortened to "Cy," in honor of the damage he'd done to the grandstand. And so it stayed, to become not only the name of the man, but also baseball's coveted pitching award.

The Tri-State League disbanded the same season Cy came on board, so he went to the Cleveland Nationals team in the fall of that same year. He won 10 and lost seven games for the team that same season. The next year, he won 27 and lost 22, and went on to post a win record above .500 for the next 13 seasons.

All in all, he won a staggering 511 games while pitching for the Cleveland Nationals, the St. Louis Cardinals, the Boston Red Sox, the Cleveland Indians and the Boston Braves.

Cy Young

He pitched two hitless shutouts, one perfect game, and pitched and won both games of a doubleheader. His best season, 1896, was 36-10. He pitched 23 consecutive hitless innings in 1904; and won 20 or more games for 14 consecutive seasons (then had two "slow seasons" and came back for two more 20-some game winners), with five of those seasons going to 36, 34, 35, 31 and 32. He also achieved 2836 strikeouts in his career, spanning 886 games.

His "perfect" game, while he was pitching for the Red Sox against Philadelphia on May 5, 1904, was the third in major league history — not a single batter got to first base.

After the 1911 season, he retired to his farm near Peoli, Ohio. Remarkably, at no point in his career did he have a sore elbow, or even require so much as a rubdown. It is said that, when he was 75, he split 3000 fenceposts for the exercise.

Cy Young died at the age of 88 in the same part of Ohio he had called home for most of his life, having set standards of achievement in his career that would become the measure of every baseball pitcher who followed.

12. HARRY VARDON
1870-1937 (Golfer)

Harry Vardon

Harry Vardon is one of the revered figures of golf. In addition to winning an all-time great six British Open championships from 1896 to 1914, he was runner up in that competition four times. Two of the wins were playoffs. In 1896, at Muirfield, in East Lothian, Scotland, he defeated John Taylor, 157 to 161 in 36 holes. In 1911, at Royal St. George's, at Sandwich, England, he won when Arnuad Massy conceded at the 35th hole.In addition, he was the champion at the US Open played at the Chicago Golf Club in Wheaton, Illinois, in 1900, defeating J.H. Taylor 313 to 315.

Later, in 1913, Vardon was a runner up after a playoff with Francis Ouimet and Ted Ray, tied at 304. Ouimet beat Vardon and Ray, 72 to 77 and 78, in 18 holes.

He was said to be a crusty man, not one to mince words. A story is told that he was playing a round with the then-18-year-old Bobby Jones (see no. 25) at Toledo, Ohio. Though later a man of grace and quiet self-control, Bobby was given to a perfection-ist's bad temper in his youth.

Vardon and Jones were playing fairly even, when the brash young Jones knocked his ball into a bunker. To assuage his own ego, Jones turned to Vardon and asked, "Did you ever see a worse shot?" Vardon spoke his first and only word of the day: "No." From that day forward, Bobby Jones learned to control his emotions.

In 1920, at age 50, and after two bouts with tuberculosis, he tied for second in the USGA open. In addition to serving the game through his work on its behalf, he also did course alterations, such as at the great Irish course, Royal County Down, in Newcastle.

Harry Vardon died at the age of 67.

13. RAY EWRY
1873-1937 (Olympic Jumper)

Ray Ewry was truly an amazing athlete, winning 10 Olympic Gold Medals (more than any other track and field athlete) in four consecutive Olympic Games — 1900, 1904, 1906 and 1908 — in the standing high jump, standing broad jump and standing triple jump.

While he is considered to be the all-time leading exponent of these events, Ewry's achievement has a deeper aspect: he was born paralyzed from the waist down.

Despite his doctor's prediction that he would never be able to walk or move about on his own, Ewry set his own exercise schedule, aiming for a progressive regimen that would help him become mobile by increments.

By determination, and years of this grueling therapy, he achieved his goal. Even so, mere mobility was not enough: he had to push on to greater heights, as if to overcome his early years altogether. In his twenties, he became the New York Athletic Club's star performer in the standing jumps.

The standing jumps were regular AAU events in Ewry's time. Often, standing-jump athletes held weights in their hands to add momentum (as did the ancient Greeks when they performed the running broad jump). The following are some of Ewry's best performances *without* weights.

In the Olympics at Paris, in July of 1906, he did a standing high jump of five feet, five inches; again, at the same games in Paris, he hit a mark in the standing hop, step and jump of 34 feet, eight-and-one-half inches. Then, on August 4, 1906, in New York City, he performed a standing broad jump of 11 feet, six inches.

While the standing jumps were discontinued from Olympic competition in 1910, Ray Ewry's record 10 Gold track and field medals lives on; and even more so does the influence of his indomitable spirit.

Ray Ewry

Modest, good-natured Honus Wagner was born **John Peter Wagner** in Carnegie, Pennsylvania on February 24, 1874. The nickname "Honus" (a variant of Hans) came later, when he was known as baseball's "Flying Dutchman."

Among his more minor accomplishments was his being the first baseball player to have an autograph series of baseball bats dedicated in his honor, courtesy of the Hillerich & Bradsby Company in 1905.

While he is unanimously accepted as the best shortstop the game has ever known, Wagner was extremely versatile, and in fact played at every position except catcher for his first five years in the major leagues.

His major accomplishments include: setting records for making the most hits, 3430; hitting the most runs, 1740; getting the most bases, 4878; leading the league the most times in batting, eight; and hitting more than .300 the most times, 17. The latter two records still stand, and are all the more remarkable in that it came *before* the present era of the comparatively short outfield and the lively ball.

He led the league in stolen bases in five separate years. His lifetime batting average was .328; his lifetime fielding average was .945.

Wagner first played with a Steubenville, Ohio team, in 1895; in 1896, he went to a team in Paterson, New Jersey, where he attracted the attention of the Louisville Colonels owner Barney Dreyfuss. Then the

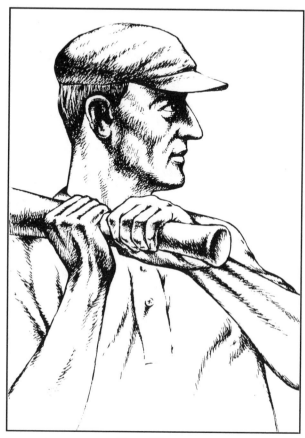

Honus Wagner

league was downsized in 1900, and Dreyfuss bought the Pittsburgh Pirates, where Wagner was to play for the following 17 years.

He was remarkable for his humility, never once arguing for more money and in fact turning down one pay raise because he felt it was too much.

He retired at age 43, and played semipro baseball for another seven or eight years, as well as managing a sporting goods store. He returned to the Pirates as a coach in 1933, serving in that capacity up to 1951. Honus Wagner died on December 6, 1955 at the age of 81.

Karl Emil Julius Ulrich Salchow was born in Stockholm, Sweden on August 7, 1877. Salchow not only set a record for winning 10 Men's World Championships, but he also invented one of figure skating's most difficult maneuvers, the Salchow jump. He won his 10 World's Championships in 1901-1905 and 1907-1911.

He was also the first to win an Olympic Gold Medal for skating, in 1908. From 1919 to 1932 he served on the Swedish Amateur Boxing Committee and from 1935 to 1937 he was president of the International Skating Union.

Ulrich Salchow

The Salchow jump is varied by the number of revolutions the skater makes: hence, "double Salchow" and "triple Salchow" can be heard among the performance evaluations during skating competitions.

In a complete Salchow, the skater takes off from the rear inside edge of one skate, completes one (or two or three, etc.) revolution(s), and lands on the rear outside edge of the other skate.

Some controversy has been generated by the increasing dominance of such difficult jumps in international competition — especially at the Winter Olympics. Some critics feel that multiple, complex jumps place a premium on sheer athleticism at the expense of grace and sublimity of style.

Ulrich Salchow died in the city of his birth, on April 19, 1949.

The great-grandson of American railway and shipping baron Cornelius Vanderbilt, **Harold Vanderbilt** had two passions — yachting and bridge (he invented contract bridge).

Yacht racing in the nineteenth and early twentieth centuries featured professional pilots. Vanderbilt changed that: he was an amateur who successfully won the **America's Cup** three times for the New York Yacht Club. Post-Vanderbilt yacht racing has seen the dominance of amateur pilots.

His crew was highly organized, each man a master of his own duties, so that the pilot shouted an order once only, and could concentrate on steering the boat. Failure to meet this mark lost one's place on the crew.

It was fitting that this new kind of pilot would command a new type of racing yacht, built in tune with a new classification for racing yachts: While all previous boats were classified, all boats in a particular competition would be of the same recognizable type, ending the "handicap" system that had been in use.

Named for their sequence in the classifications, the new "J" boats were to have 75-87 foot waterlines, and feature single, massive triangular mainsails with overlapping jibs (and, later on, a parachute spinnaker as well).

Vanderbilt proposed further innovations on the 80-foot-long *Enterprise*, the J-boat he would pilot to win his first America's Cup in 1930, including a unique "Park Avenue" boom, with runners and slides that would allow aerodynamic shaping of the mainsail; a 162-foot mainmast made of two hollow tubes of lightweight duralumin, half the weight of a conventional mast; a unique double centerboard, to help both in sailing into the wind, *and* in running before the wind; and below decks, more than two dozen winches to handle the ship's lines.

Enterprise beat Irish tea merchant Sir Thomas Lipton's *Shamrock V* in the 1930 race, four straight races in a row (the cup went to the best four out of seven). In 1934, *Enterprise* was made obsolete by international sympathy against her below-decks winches and double centerboard.

A new boat had to be built. This was *Rainbow*. The competition this time was Englishman Thomas Sopwith, of aeronautics fame. His J-boat, *Endeavour*, was faster than *Rainbow*, but due to a strike, he replaced his entire crew two weeks before the race. *Rainbow* won, four races to two.

The greatest J-boat was Vanderbilt's *Ranger*, which due to the growing Depression, was built at cost by a shipyard, and fitted with rigging from Vanderbilt's two previous J-boats. In 1937, *Ranger* defended the America's Cup against Tom Sopwith's *Endeavour II*, winning four in a row, by 17, 18, four and three minutes, respectively.

The deepening Depression, the advent of World War II, and the after-war tax structure spelled the end for the extravagant J-boats. Harold Vanderbilt had "piloted" a landmark era in yachting.

Harold Vanderbilt

17. TY COBB
1887-1961 (Baseball Player)

Tyrus Raymond "Ty" Cobb first played with the Augusta team in the South Atlantic League (where Grantland Rice had noticed him and tagged him with his career-long nickname, "The Georgia Peach"), and was then bought by the Detroit Tigers in August of 1905.

While his first Detroit year saw him batting .240, the remaining 22 years of his career featured a sustained batting average of .322 or better, going over the .400 mark in three of those seasons, for a record-setting career batting average of .367.

One year he stole 96 bases, and in fact had a career record of 892 steals. He batted left and threw right. He won the Batting Championship a record 12 times, amassed 4191 base hits, a number exceeded only by Pete Rose (4256). He made 200+ hits in nine seasons, hit 297 triples, scored 118 home runs, and played in 2940 major league games.

He was a legendary base stealer, sometimes stealing home on a run from first on an infield out. He played in a rough and tough era, when spiking was common, pitchers were allowed to use any trick they could muster, and for more than half of his career, the sluggish "dead ball" was in use.

He was the first player to win the Home Run Championship, achieve the highest batting average, and amass the most runs batted in, in one season — 1909. He was also the first player inducted into the Baseball Hall of Fame. Another mark of notoriety: his temper was such that he fought with fans, officials, and with his own teammates. He also practiced his own advice, freely given to players of another generation: "Practice what you're not good at."

In 1920, Cobb took on the job of player/manager for the Tigers, but resigned that position in 1926. In 1927, he went with Connie Mack's Athletics, and played through 1928, still batting .323.

Through shrewd investment over the years, he had become a millionaire, and he continued to hunt and hike. He died on July 17, 1961, in Atlanta, Georgia.

Ty Cobb

18. JIM THORPE
1888-1953 (All-Around Athlete)

Jim Thorpe

In 1950, an Associated Press poll named him the Greatest Athlete of the First Half of the Century (with 879 points versus runner-up **Babe Ruth [see no. 21]** at 579), and the Greatest Football Player of the First Half of the Century (over **Red Grange [see no. 27]**). At the Olympic Games in 1912, the King of Sweden said to him what most of the world was thinking: "Sir, you are the greatest athlete in the world."

James Francis Thorpe was a master of all sports save golf, croquet and tennis. He could high-jump six feet five inches; he pole-vaulted 11 feet; ran the 100-yard dash in 10 flat; the 220 in 21.8; the 440 in 50.8; threw the discus 136 feet; the javelin 163 feet; the hammer 140 feet; ran the mile in 4:35; the 220 low hurdles in 24; and the 120 high hurdles in 15 seconds.

Part Irish, part Welsh and part Sac and Fox Indian, he was born on May 28, 1888 in Prague, Oklahoma, where he rode horses, hunted, and chased his dogs through the woods and underbrush. After his twin brother, Charles, died of pneumonia, Thorpe went to the Carlisle Indian School in Pennsylvania, where he was to make his name in football and track.

Although he was remembered for his Olympic accomplishments, his real love was football. He kicked field goals up to 79 yards, and once completed two back-to-back field-length ball returns. He kicked well, he ran well, he passed well, he blocked well. He was an unstoppable ball carrier, telling the opposing linemen *exactly* where he would go through, leaving the field strewn with would-be tacklers. Thorpe was the deciding factor in the Carlisle Indian School's domination of the best college teams of its era.

By the 1911 season, he was a halfback on Walter Camp's All-America football team. He next went on to win the gold for the pentathlon (scoring 8412 out of a possible 10,000 points) and decathlon in the 1912 Olympics, but it was discovered that he had played baseball for money during a break from school. He had to give his medals back.

Thorpe joined the New York Giants in 1913, but he ran afoul of the manager, and was sent to the minors, only to be recalled for the World Series of 1913. He eventually played for the Cincinnati Reds and the Boston Bees, quitting baseball in 1915, to play for the Canton Bulldogs pro football team, for a then-lordly $500 per game.

In 1920, the **American Professional Football Association** (it became the National Football League in 1922) was established, and Thorpe was its first president. He remained an active player, retiring in 1930, when he fell upon hard times, began to drink heavily, and suffered obscurity despite repeated attempts on the part of interested citizens to get his Olympic medals restored. He served in the Merchant Marine during World War II, and died of a heart attack in 1953. The Olympic Committee relented in 1983, and restored Jim Thorpe's medals at long last.

19. TAZIO NUVOLARI
1892-1953 (Auto Racer)

His driving was legendary. He invented the four-wheel drift, to compensate for his small size versus the gargantuan, hard-to-steer race cars of his day. He won 30 of the most important races run in Europe between 1921 and 1939. **Tazio Nuvolari** drove in 172 races, and won 64 of them, placed second 16 times and third nine times against the toughest competition of his time, at a time when it was a feat simply to *keep one's car together long enough to finish the race.*

It was said that if Nuvolari's car was as fast as the competition, and stayed in one piece for the race, he would probably win; if it were 10 miles an hour slower, he could still win.

He won the grueling and dangerous Mille Miglia (Thousand Miles) race twice, but perhaps his greatest feat was accomplished in the 1935 Grand Prix of Germany. Driving an aging red Alfa-Romeo, Nuvolari was up against the fastest race cars in the world, the 180 mph Auto-Union cars; and the 175 mph Mercedes Benzes, driven by some of the best drivers in Europe. His Alfa was 20 mph slower.

It was a mountain course with 175 curves, measuring 14 miles per lap. By the tenth lap, Nuvolari had risen from sixth to first place. Then, his crew bungled a refueling stop, dropping him back to sixth. By the thirteenth lap, Nuvolari had regained second, and was pushing the first place car, a Mercedes driven by Von Brauchitsch, so hard, that the Mercedes ran its tires ragged, had a blowout halfway through the last lap, and Nuvolari roared on to win by 32 seconds.

His tremendous drive to win was such that he once ran in a motorcycle race fresh from the hospital, in a head-to-toe cast. He had split-second reactions, enabling him to escape trouble as it was happening. Perhaps this is the reason that he was one of the few European race car drivers of his generation to live long enough to die in bed.

He contracted tuberculosis during World War II, but still drove seven times in 1946, winning the Grand Prix of Albi. In 1947, he drove for Ferrari, and won twice, but the tuberculosis made him hypersensitive to racing fuel. His lungs hemorraged.

Even so, he almost won the Mille Miglia a third time, when water in his magneto slowed his car within sight of the finish line, and the second place man passed him; he himself finished second. In 1948, he was 30 minutes ahead of the others in the Mille when his Ferrari broke down. In 1950, he won at Monte Pellegrino, but had to be lifted out of his car, spitting blood. He died on August 11, 1953, and was buried with his helmet and his steering wheel.

Tazio Nuvolari

26

20. BILL TILDEN
1893-1953 (Tennis Player)

He was one of the greatest players tennis has ever known. Unanimously named "The Greatest Player of the First Half of the Twentieth Century," in a poll taken by the United Press in 1950, **William Tatem Tilden, Jr.** had entered his first tournament at the age of eight — nothing unusual for a youth in the Philadelphia Main Line suburb of Germantown at the time: Tennis was part of growing up. Though he won the match, Bill preferred to read and listen to music.

Not until he was 20 did his interest in tennis really turn into a vocation. The US Women's Singles champion, Mary K. Browne, saw him practicing on a grass court, and was impressed by his ability. Browne asked him to team up with her for the National Mixed Doubles Championship, and they won it. Tilden was elated, and decided that tennis would be his life's work.

Bill Tilden

Tilden played in his first national championship game in 1916, losing. In 1918, he made it to the final round, only to lose to R. Linley Murray; Tilden then teamed with 15-year-old Vincent Richards to win the Men's Doubles.

By then, Tilden had made enough of a reputation to add drama to his historic series of confrontations with arch-rival William Johnston, of California. Johnston's powerful forehand shots were pitted against Tilden's rocketlike, flat service.

In 1919, Tilden beat Johnston on the grass at Newport, and won in the East-West championships. Johnston beat Tilden in the clay court championships, and devastated him in the US Championships at Forest Hills. Tilden's weak backhand had betrayed him.

This caused Tilden to take the winter off, concentrating on strengthening his backhand. Tilden returned to the sport in 1920, becoming the first American to win the **Wimbledon Championship** (despite a knee tendon injury), and defeating Johnston in one of tennis's greatest matches (6-1, 1-6, 7-5, 5-7, 6-3), at Forest Hills the same year.

From that point on, Tilden achieved a dominance previously unknown in the sport. Until his retirement from competitive tennis in 1933, he won seven US Amateur Championships; three Wimbledons; 31 national championships (singles, doubles and mixed doubles, indoors and outdoors); was ranked Number One US Amateur 10 times; in Davis Cup competition from 1920-25, was unbeaten in singles play and lost only one doubles match; and played on the Davis Cup team for 11 years.

Tilden remained active as an instructor in Beverly Hills, and tried his hand at writing novels and screenplays. In 1951 he played a tournament at Cleveland, and was planning to play another when he died of a heart attack on June 5, 1953.

27

21. BABE RUTH
1895-1948 (Baseball Player)

Babe Ruth

He was perhaps the greatest baseball player of all time. He is also credited as being the man who helped baseball to recover a favorable image after the dreadful "Black Sox" scandal in which players of the Chicago White Sox took bribes to lose games.

George Herman "Babe" Ruth had an enormous impact on the game. The 1920s is often referred to as the "Ruth Era," just as Yankee Stadium was tagged "The House the Ruth Built."

Because fans flocked to watch him hit home runs, major league owners invented the "live ball," and outlawed a whole battery of pitchers' tricks so that more players would hit homers. Soon, batting styles throughout the league changed to take advantage of the new ball and the new rules.

But he was a great all-around player, too. In fact, Babe began his career as a left-handed pitcher with the Red Sox in 1915. He won 89 of 158 games, with a stretch of 29 consecutive scoreless innings, an earned run average of 2.28, and a 3-0 win record in the 1914-1916 **World Series**.

Although he was a great pitcher, the Sox switched him to outfield because they wanted to be able to use him as a power hitter every game. Even so, the Yankees traded for him in 1919, and with them he really launched into his career. The Yankees played him in the outfield, too.

Nicknamed "the Sultan of Swat," he hit a record 54 homers his first year in New York, with a .375 batting average; he hit 59 home runs in 1921; and then 60 in 1927; he led the American League in home runs for 12 years. His record of 714 total career home runs was not eclipsed until **Henry Aaron (see no. 52)** did so in 1974.

Ruth and teammate **Lou Gehrig (1903-1942)** were a batting pair that powered the Yankees to the World Series seven times in the period 1921-32. While he had a reputation for wild living, he answered a plea that he become a better role model for the kids who adored him by reforming his ways, and kept his pledge until his death in June of 1948.

He was a gentle man outside the boxing ring — but when he donned his gloves, he became "The Manassa Mauler," doing a rhythmic, shuffling dance, and humming an almost inaudible tune, whose beat was the cadence of his punches.

Born **William Harrison Dempsey** in the mining town of Manassa, Colorado, Dempsey was working full shifts in the mines by the time he reached his teens. He wanted to be a fighter, and set out on his own, fighting in the back rooms of saloons. In 1917, he linked up with manager Jack "Doc" Kearns, who arranged fights with top-ranked heavyweights with Dempsey.

He won 21 fights (17 by knockouts) in 1918. In 1919, Dempsey, at 187 pounds, fought 245-pound Jess Willard for the championship. He knocked Willard down seven times in the first round, and by the third round, Willard conceded defeat. While Dempsey's manager — bitter after court battles with Dempsey — later claimed he had loaded Dempsey's gloves with plaster of Paris, sportswriters have since tested that theory and found that the plaster would have *softened* Dempsey's blows, if anything.

Then followed title-defense knockouts of Billy Miske and Billy Brennan. Dempsey was also bucking a charge that he had dodged the draft in World War I — something he was finally cleared of in court. In 1921, however, the crafty Kearns used this to build the first million-dollar ($1,626,580) prizefight, between Dempsey and war hero Georges Carpentier. Carpentier went down in four rounds.

Then came a nondescript 15-round decision over the fading heavyweight Tommy Gibbons. That same year, 1923, saw the most ferocious heavyweight title fight of the century. Luis Firpo, "the Bull of the Pampas," was matched against Dempsey. Firpo dropped Dempsey seconds into the fight. Dempsey responded by knocking Firpo down six times. Firpo then knocked Dempsey out of the ring for a nine-count. Dempsey dropped Firpo once more before the bell. Round two saw Dempsey floor Firpo twice, the second time being the knockout.

In 1926, Dempsey made his sixth and last title defense, against Gene Tunney. Tunney stayed away from Dempsey, out-boxing the champion, who was hampered by three years of inactivity. Tunney won the decision. The return bout, one year later, saw Dempsey knock Tunney down for the famous "long count." Tunney was actually down for 14 seconds, but Dempsey failed to return to a neutral corner, and the count was delayed, giving Tunney ample time to recover.

Jack Dempsey epitomized boxing for America with his rough, tough, knock-em-out style. He was in fact voted "The Best Boxer of the Half-Century" by an Associated Press poll in 1950.

Jack went on to represent the boxing sport as a public figure, and to referee some bouts. He also opened a famous restaurant in New York City — "Jack Dempsey's," where anyone could walk in and shake hands with "the Champ."

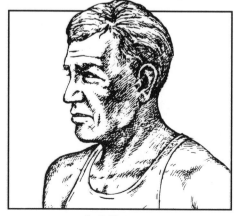

Jack Dempsey

23. ROGERS HORNSBY
1896-1963 (Baseball Player)

Considered by many to be the greatest right-handed hitter of all time, **Rogers "Rajah" Hornsby** was born in Winters, Texas in 1896. Hornsby still holds the all-time record for career batting average: .358 over 23 years, one year longer than **Ty Cobb (see no. 17)**. He also hit .400 three times, including a single-season record .424 in 1924. His cold impassive stare imtimidated pitchers, and umpires as well.

There is a story of a pitcher who put three perfect strikes over the plate against Hornsby and complained to the umpire who called them as balls.

"Young fellow," replied the umpire, "Mr. Hornsby will let you know when you throw a strike."

He led the National League in batting seven times, including six years in a row, 1920-25, with averages of .370, .397, .401, .384, .424, .403; and .387 in 1928, with Boston. This was no easy feat of dominance in "the Age of Ruth," but serves to emphasize what an outstanding batsman he was. He did not become as much of a media star as **Babe Ruth (see no. 21)** because he was cool rather than flamboyant and the New York press loved the Babe's man-about-town high jinks.

Hornsby managed — as well as playing with — the St. Louis Cardinals to a 4-3 win in the 1926 World Series. He also managed the Braves, Cubs, Browns and Cincinnati Reds. He was also a two-time Most Valuable Player in 1925 and 1929.

He played second base for the Cardinals from 1915-26; the New York Giants in 1927; the Boston Braves in 1928; the Chicago Cubs from 1929-32; the Cardinals again in 1933; and the St. Louis Browns from 1933-37. Elected to the Hall of Fame in 1942, he died in 1963.

Rogers Hornsby

24. PAAVO NURMI
1897-1973 (Runner)

Paavo Nurmi

Paavo Johannes Nurmi was the first long-distance runner to plan his race scientifically, often carrying a stopwatch in practice and in his more important races, with which he would time his progress, throwing the watch away as he began his last lap. Before him, runners would usually simply jog up until the last two laps, and then pour all they had into the finish.

Nurmi established a methodology that is in use even today, when more advanced timing methods are used. He won nine Olympic Gold medals (six as an individual, three as part of a team) and three silvers in the Olympic Games of 1920, 1924 and 1928.

He set 23 world records from 1921-1931 in events ranging from the 1500 to the 20,000 meter runs.

He was born in Abo, Finland on June 13, 1897. His family was poor, and he had to work from the time he was 12. Still, he showed promise as a runner. Then came World War I, and he became a soldier. Yet he continued his running discipline, slipping out in the early morning, running miles along the icy roads and returning in time for reveille.

At war's end, Nurmi began systematic note taking, comparing his time with other runners' times, and calculating exactly at what points in a given race to simply stride, and when to run fastest.

In the 1920 Olympics, he lost his first race, but quickly rebounded and won. In June 1921, he set world records for the 10,000 meters (30:40.2) and for the six miles (28:41.2). In the next two years, he added three more records — 5000 meters (14:35.2); 1500 meters (3:52.6) and the mile (4:10.4).

In the 1924 Olympic Games in Paris, he won in the 1500-meter race, the 5500-meter race, the cross-country race and the 3000-meter team race establishing himself as more dominant than any previous runner, especially in light of the fact that the 1500 and the 5500 were run a mere 55 minutes apart! Even more amazing, Nurmi had run a 1500 and a 5500 race in the same schedule two weeks before the Olympics, and bettered his own world records in both — two new world records within one hour.

At the 1928 Olympics, he won the 10,000, for his second 10,000 meter Gold over an eight-year span — a feat of resiliency and endurance without precedent. He went on to set records in distance running up to July, 1931, when he set his last — two miles in 8:59.5.

Paavo Nurmi won his last race at the Finnish National Championships in 1933, triumphing in the 1500. He continues to be a revered Finnish national sports figure.

25. BOBBY JONES
1902-1971 (Golfer)

Bobby Jones

He remains the only man to ever win golfing's Grand Slam — which he did at the age of 28, by winning the US Open, the British Open, the US Amateur and the British Amateur championships in 1930. All in all, he won four US Opens (1923, 1926, 1929 and 1930); three British Opens (1926, 1927 and 1930); five US Amateurs (1924, 1925, 1927, 1928 and 1930); and played in six Walker Cups.

He did all of this as an amateur, often playing against the best professionals — and winning. Especially noteworthy, the Scots, a notably golf-oriented people, adopted him as one of their own, and thronged the fairways whenever he visited and took to the courses.

He was born **Robert Tyre Jones, Jr.**, on March 17, 1902, in Atlanta, Georgia and took up golf when his parents moved near the Atlanta Athletic Club. By the age of nine, he was the AAC's junior champion. He was 14 when he entered his first US Amateur tournament. He won in the first and second rounds but lost the final to Robert Gardner, the defending champion.

He was burdened with a short temper in his youth, but help from his colleagues, especially a pithy comment from the legendary **Harry Vardon (see no. 12)**, helped Bobby to establish the self-control and refinement for which he is noted.

Jones was to struggle over the years, until, in 1924, he had the realization that, in match play, he was worrying too much about his competitor: He decided from then on to play against the par, not the competition. That year, he won his first US Amateur. He also married his high-school sweetheart.

His feats include a round of golf that has been described as perfect as humanly possible — during the British Open of 1926; par was 72: He made 66, divided evenly going out and coming back. He had six fours and three threes on each nine, or 33 putts and 33 other strokes.

In 1928, he joined his father's law firm, but continued golf as a serious pursuit. When he won the Grand Slam in 1930, he retired, preferring to remain an advocate of the game. He established the Masters Tournament in 1934, building a magnificent golf course to host it, the Augusta National Golf Course, in Augusta, Georgia. Bobby Jones remained an active and revered proponent of the game. In 1940 he was named to the PGA Hall of Fame, and in 1972 after his death, he was elected to the World Hall of Fame.

She won a record six US Women's Amateur titles, in 1922, 1925, 1928, 1929, 1930 and 1935, and was hailed as the "the **Bobby Jones (see no. 25)** of women's golf."

She grew up as **Glenna Collett** in Providence, Rhode Island, adding the family name Vare when she married Edwin Vare in her young adulthood. Her father was a practiced golfer, and as a child, she often accompanied him to the Metacomet Golf Club in Providence. Soon, she was playing golf, too — and because of her rapidly maturing ability, was allowed to play the course.

Bobby Jones commented on her by saying, "It is especially a treat to watch Glenna Collett. Her accuracy with the spoon and brassie is to me the most important part of her well-rounded game."

She entered her first major golfing competition at the age of 17.

How could she have known, then, that she would become a legend, and would still be winning at the age of 56 — the age at which she won the Rhode Island State Championship for the last time? (She won it for the first time 37 years earlier, in 1922.) She won 49 amateur championships in 18 years and 19 consecutive matches from 1928 to 1931.

Among her most famous accomplishments was winning her sixth National Amateur title in 1935, after a two-year retirement to have children. She was playing against such younger luminaries as Marian McDougal, Betty Jameson and **Patty Berg (see no. 37)**. This was her fourteenth national tournament, and she prevailed, on a cold, rainy day that was remarkable for the 15,000-spectator gallery that turned out to watch the legendary Glenna Collett Vare win the tournament.

She blazed a path for other women golfers to follow. Never again would women golfers be thought of with anything but respect as athletes.

Glenna Collett-Vare

27. RED GRANGE
1903-1991 (Football Player)

Red Grange

Harold Edward "Red" Grange was also nicknamed "The Galloping Ghost" for his elusive but aggressive running style as a halfback. He was a three-time All-American at Illinois. His college career record was 2071 yards over three seasons in just 388 carries, for an average of 5.3 yards per carry; 31 touchdowns; and six scoring passes.

He was born on June 13, 1903, in Forksville, Pennsylvania, but he grew up in Wheaton, Illinois. Perhaps it was only natural he'd play for Illinois when of college age. Probably his most famous exploit as a college player came in 1924, when Illinois faced Michigan, an undefeated powerhouse of a team.

Grange rushed for 265 yards and four touchdowns in the *first 12 minutes* of the game. All in all, he compiled 402 yards of offense, 64 yards passing, and five touchdowns to help Illinois win, 39-14.

On Thanksgiving day, 1925, he was talked into joining the Chicago Bears pro football team. His hiring before graduation day prompted a controversy that led to the adoption of the draft system, whereby graduation from college had to be achieved before football contracts could be signed.

Grange stayed with the Bears, and from November to February, 1926, he earned $100,000, the highest salary a pro football player had earned to that point. His presence gave the NFL credibility with the public it sorely needed to gain widespread acceptance of pro football as an honorable game.

Unprecedented crowds came to pro games featuring Grange. He played two seasons following that with the New York Yankees pro football team, then returned to the Bears from 1929-34, and took part in the NFL's first championship game (in 1933): Chicago beat New York 23-21, in a contest that was tied six times.

He then tried his hand as an assistant coach, and then turned to less sports-oriented pursuits like acting. He returned to football as a radio and television commentator on college and pro football games, especially focusing on the Bears. In 1961, he retired to Florida, where he had business interests in insurance, real estate and an orange grove. He died of pneumonia on January 28, 1991.

28. HELEN WILLS MOODY
b. 1905 (Tennis Player)

Helen Wills was born in Centerville, California in 1905, and was to undertake a career that astonished the world. Her record of eight Wimbledon singles titles was not broken until 1990. She also won three Wimbledon doubles titles. She won a record seven US National Singles Championships and four Doubles Championships; she played in 10 Wightman Cup matches, winning 18 out of 20 singles contests. She also was the only American woman to win an Olympic Gold Medal for tennis in 1924.

She did all this between 1923 and 1938. As a young girl, her father had encouraged her to play tennis. At 14, she beat him for the first time, and he got her a membership in the Berkeley Tennis Club, where she won the Pacific Coast Juniors; at 15, she won the National Juniors title; and at 16, made it into the finals of the Nationals at Forest Hills.

At 17, in 1923, she defeated Molla Mallory 62-61 to win the Nationals. She was to become as noted for her refusal to drink or smoke as for her leading the bandwagon for more athletic attire (versus heavy, long skirts and long sleeves) for women tennis players.

"I aim for the all-round game ... good net and backcourt play, development of all strokes ... the player should be at home wherever she may be on the court."

Helen Wills Moody

William Benjamin Hogan was born on August 13, 1912 in Dublin, Texas, the son of a blacksmith. His father died when he was 10, and the family moved to Fort Worth. Ben had to sell newspapers to keep them in food; at 12, he switched to caddying at Glen Garden Country Club, and thus the career of the "greatest golf shot maker who ever lived" had its start.

Hogan was a businesslike craftsman on the course during his heyday. From 1946 to 1953, he won four US Opens, two Masters, two PGA Tournaments and the only British Open he had ever competed in. He was named PGA Player of the Year four times. Three of these victories combined in a near-grand slam for Hogan in 1953: that was the year he won the Masters, the US Open and the British Open.

On February 2, 1949, he and his wife Valerie were driving home to Fort Worth, Texas, when a huge bus went out of control and careened into their lane. Hogan instinctively threw himself across the seat to protect his wife. Valerie sustained minor injuries and Ben suffered a double fracture of the pelvis, a broken collarbone, a broken left ankle and a broken rib.

There was doubt he'd rise to professional heights again. Yet this heroic and determined man came back. In January 1950, he battled "Slammin'" Sammy Snead into a playoff in the Los Angeles Open. Five months later, Hogan beat Lloyd Mangrum and George Fazio in a playoff to the Golden Anniversary Open.

Nine months later, he won the 1951 Masters, and then won the US Open. In 1953, he swept three major tournaments. Dubbed "The Hawk" by his competitors, Hogan was often distant, but never discourteous. In spite of his seeming steely nature, he was well-liked.

The great Gene Sarazen said of him, "From tee to green, there never was anyone to compare with Hogan ... If he had been able to putt as well as **Bobby Jones (see no. 25)** or **Jack Nicklaus (see no. 60)**, no one could have come close to him. Yet he was such a superb shot maker that his putting was never put to too severe a test."

Ben Hogan

She was born on April 8, 1912 in Oslo, Norway, the second child of a fur merchant who indulged his children. Sonja got her first pair of skates at the age of eight. Her innate ability was so evident that her father paid for the best instruction in skating for her.

She won her first Norwegian National title at the age of 10, in 1924. **Sonja Henie** entered her first Olympic Games at the age of 12. She also won Scandinavian championships in tennis and skiing. Her skills at horseback riding, sprinting and swimming also earned her fame.

But her skating was beyond all else. From 1927 to 1936, she won 10 world championships; she also won three consecutive Olympic Gold Medals (1928, 1932, 1936). In all, she won nearly 1500 competitions — *and* she became a Hollywood movie star in 11 Darryl F. Zanuch 20th Century-Fox extravaganzas.

She turned a sport that was reserved for the very rich and for those who lived in ice-bound countries into a sport for everybody. Ice rinks suddenly sprung up all over the Western Hemisphere, with thousands of would-be imitators slipping and falling all over themselves — and having a great time.

Sonja Henie

Ice dancing became a popular pastime. Her films inspired future Olympic champions like Ludmila and Oleg Protopopov (1964-1968 Olympic Pairs Skating Gold Medalists) to don skates for the first time.

She had become one of her era's most intriguing figures — one of the very few sports stars who have made their sport resonate with a kind of magic that communicates with men and women in all walks of life.

She died of leukemia in 1969. She had made approximately $47 million with all her ventures.

Sonja Henie will be remembered as much for her brilliant athletic career as for her brilliant charm at communicating the *thrill* of what she was doing with two steel blades and an arena covered with glorious *ice*.

Born in Danville, Alabama on September 12, 1913, his family moved nine years later to Cleveland, Ohio, where **James Cleveland "JC" Owens** underwent a name change because of a schoolteacher's bad hearing. His new name was "Jesse." At 13, he ran in his first track and field race.

By the time he was in high school, he was a nationally-known sprinter. He then went to Ohio State University, paying his way as a night elevator operator. In May 1935, he was a sophomore, getting ready for his first Big Ten track meet. He and his roommate were fooling around, mock-wrestling, when Jesse slipped and fell down a flight of stairs, wrenching his back so badly that he couldn't work or practice for the entire week.

Rather than withdraw from the meet, Jesse vowed to "give it a try event by event." On May 25, 1935, in the 45 minutes from 3:15 p.m. to 4:00 p.m., Jesse Owens tied the world record for the 100-yard dash (9.4 seconds); set a new world record for the broad jump (26 feet, 8.25 inches, which stood for 25 years); broke the world record for the 220-yard dash — and simultaneously did same for the for the 200 meter dash (20.3 seconds); and broke the world record for the 220-yard low hurdles — which also broke the record for the 200-meter low hurdles (22.6 seconds).

It was a feat of record-setting that has not been equalled.

Owens is also famed for his sparkling performance at the 1936 **Olympic Games** in Berlin — not only an athletic triumph, but a political tweaking of Adolph Hitler's racist policies. Hitler believed that this Olympics was the perfect forum to demonstrate his theory that the Aryan race is superior to all others. The Nazis ridiculed the United States for having black men on the US Olympic Team. When it was all over,

six of the 11 individual Gold medals won by the US were won by these same men.

Owens himself won the 100-meter dash in 10.3 seconds; the 200-meter in 20.7; and the broad jump at 26 feet and one-half inch. In doing so, he broke two Olympic records and almost broke a third. Also, he led the US relay team that won the 400-meter relay in 39.8 seconds, a new world record.

A grim-faced Adolf Hitler left the stadium before Jesse was awarded his third Gold Medal. Ironically, Owens returned to the United States and suffered for years from the incipient racism in his own country.

Always the competitor, though, he triumphed again, running a successful public relations firm of his own. Jesse Owens died on March 31, 1980.

Jesse Owens

In addition to being perhaps the greatest 14-1 "straight pool" champion the sport has ever known, **Willie Mosconi** did more than any other man to popularize pocket billiards.

Mosconi dominated pocket billiards. He was World Pocket Billiard Champion in 1940, 1942-1943, 1944-1946, 1947-1948 and 1950-58, retiring from competition while still holding the title.

His records include: Exhibition High Run, 527 balls (1945); High Run during a game, 127 (1946); High Run in tournament play, 150 (1956); Most Consecutive Games won in tournament play, 14; and more. In 1957-1958, he established records for High Grand Average of 2000 points at 15.85; and of 1350 points at 19.

He served as a technical advisor in the production of the 1961 Paul Newman-Jackie Gleason film, "The Hustler," a picture that made the nickname of pool shark Rudolph Walderone — i.e., "Minnesota Fats" — a household word in the United States. In 1978, NBC's "Wide World of Sports" featured an exhibition match between Mosconi and "Fats," and Mosconi easily trounced his opponent.

Known for his serious, almost scholarly concentration on his sport, and his impeccable attire, Mosconi established an image of the pocket billiards champion as a figure of considerable skill and finesse.

He wrote several books explaining the sport, and was a willing advisor to many youthful contenders. Mosconi died of a heart attack in Haddon Heights, New Jersey on September 12, 1993.

Willie Mosconi

33. JOE DiMAGGIO
b. 1914 (Baseball Player)

Joseph Paul DiMaggio was born on November 25, 1914 in Martinez, California, one of nine children. He began playing sandlot ball, eventually joining the San Francisco Seals of the Pacific Coast League as a shortstop. His first full season, 1933, he played right field, and as a batter hit .340, with 28 home runs and 169 RBIs. He also hit successfully in 69 consecutive games.

In 1934, DiMaggio batted .398, with 34 homers and 154 RBIs. That same season, the New York Yankees traded for him. He played center field for the Yankees so well that he is now considered to be the best to have ever played the position.

He would lead the Yankees to 10 World Series wins in his 13 seasons with them and he was a three-time Most Valuable Player in 1939, 1940 and 1947. He led the American League in batting average (1939, .381; and 1940, .352), home runs and RBIs two times each. His most famous exploit was setting the major league record at getting a safe hit in each of 56 consecutive games.

The "Streak" started on May 15, 1941, and continued until July 17. His record for that period was: 91 hits, .408 average, 56 runs, 55 RBIs, 15 home runs hit, 21 walks and seven strikeouts. It was a national event: People who had never liked baseball became fans because of the "Streak," its mystique and the power it had to take worried

minds off the gathering clouds of World War II.

Always a gracious, nice guy, Joe DiMaggio retired from baseball in 1951, as the most popular player since **Babe Ruth (see no. 21)**. In 1957, he was inducted into the Hall of Fame. Along the way, there was a lot of interest in his brief marriage to Marilyn Monroe.

"The Yankee Clipper" did some coaching, including 1969-1970 with the Oakland A's. In 1969, he was named as Baseball's Greatest Living Player, as well as All-Time Greatest Center Fielder.

Joe DiMaggio

Born on June 26, 1914, in Port Arthur, Texas, **Mildred Ella Didrikson** was the daughter of a Norwegian ship carpenter. As a girl she worked out with apparatus constructed from clothes lines and her mother's flatirons. She got her nickname, "Babe," after hitting multiple home runs in a baseball game. It was an allusion, of course, to **Babe Ruth (see no. 21)**.

In many respects, "Babe" Didrikson was a determined athlete. In 1930, when she was 16 years old, she won the world record in Javelin with a throw of 133 feet, 3 1/4 inches.

During her career, she was chosen Female Athlete of the Year six times from 1932-1954 by the Associated Press. She won two Gold Medals, in the javelin and the 80-meter hurdles in the 1932 Olympic Games, and also won a Silver in the high jump (which would have been a Gold, but Babe's "diving" jump style was disapproved of, even though she had the height to win).

Babe Didrikson Zaharias

In 1935, she took up golf, practicing 16 hours on weekend days, and getting to the course for practice at the crack of dawn for weekday practice. She drove an estimated 1000 balls per day to sharpen her game. Her average distance off the tee was 240 yards.

She went on to win 55 pro and amateur events, including three US Open championships among the 10 major tournaments she won. She was a guiding force in the formation of the Ladies Professional Golf Association, in 1949.

She was chosen as "Female Athlete of the Half Century" by an Associated Press poll, in 1950. All this from a woman who began her career with the notion to "become the best athlete ever." As early as 1932, she won the National Amateur Athletic Union track meet by winning five events and tying for a sixth. She was the sole member of the Employers Casualty Company of Dallas: she was the team.

She loved her mother and father with great devotion, just as she shared a very soft-hearted relationship with her huge husband, the wrestler George Zaharias, whom she met on a golf course in 1937. Over the years, her sharp, unpolished demeanor of her youth gave way to a growing sophistication as she took on her new role as one of the century's most noted public figures.

With exhibitions and championship wins, she was earning in excess of $100,000 per year. She also wrote instructional articles for magazines, and penned one book, *Championship Golf*.

She had a bout with cancer in the early 1950s, and 10 months after an operation in April 1953, she recovered to win a Women's Open tournament in Miami. She capped this by winning the US Women's Open in 1954, by 12 strokes. Unfortunately, the disease returned. Babe Zaharias died of cancer on September 27, 1956.

35. JOE LOUIS
1914-1981 (Boxer)

Joe Louis

Born on May 13, 1914, near Lafayette, Alabama, **Joseph "Joe" Louis** did odd jobs as a teen, and attended Bronson Vocational School as a cabinetmaker before taking up amateur boxing. He lost his first bout to Johnny Miller, but in 1934, he won the Amateur Athletic Union Light Heavyweight championship. His record as an amateur was 43 knockout victories in 54 fights.

He fought his first professional fight on July 4, 1934, winning over Jack Kraken with a knockout (KO) in the first round. He had 25 more fights in 1934-1935. Among his fallen opponents were ex-champs Primo Carnera and Max Baer. In 1936, he fought Max Schmeling, whom Adolf Hitler touted as an example of Aryan superiority. Schmeling KO'd Louis in 12 rounds, taking advantage of a habitual flaw in Louis' defenses. A rematch was scheduled for June 22, 1938.

In the meanwhile, he KO'd the existing champ, Jimmy Braddock, in 1937. When Schmeling met Louis the second time, he was fighting the Heavyweight Champion — who had patched the chink in his defenses. Louis pounded Schmeling so fiercely in the two minutes and four seconds the fight lasted, that the crushed Schmeling had to spend time in a local hospital before going back to Germany.

He was an unobtrusive, polite man, which was reflected by his plodding style in the ring. Fighters with a lot of footwork and technical brilliance didn't bother him. As he said before defeating the speedy Billy Conn on June 18, 1941, "He can run but he can't hide." Louis was a slugger — one of the best that had ever lived.

His 11-year, eight-month (1937-1949) reign as World Heavyweight Champion remains the longest in the history of his division. His professional record was 63 wins, three losses with 49 knockouts — five of these KOs in the first round. Louis became known as "the Brown Bomber" during World War II, reflecting his status as a national figure.

He defended his title 25 times, and only three of these bouts went the full 15 rounds. In 1940-1941, he defended his title once per month — a sustained rate that no other fighter has attempted. This came to be known as Louis's "Bum of the Month" campaign. He won them all.

Joe Louis joined the US Army in 1942, staging boxing exhibitions for the soldiers until 1945. In all, he travelled 21,000 miles on the troop entertainment trail, staging 96 exhibitions during this time. He came back after the war to beat Billy Conn a second time, on June 19, 1946, in eight rounds.

He defended his title three more times, including twice against Jersey Joe Walcott, and then retired as undefeated champion on March 1, 1949. He tried a comeback two years later, lost two bouts (one to **Rocky Marciano [see no. 41]**), and gave up the gloves.

His later years were sometimes tumultuous, including a scrape with the Internal Revenue Service, three marriages and serving as an advisor to **Muhammad Ali (see no. 64)**. He died on April 12, 1981.

36. MARION LADEWIG
b. 1914 (Bowler)

Known as the greatest woman bowler of all time, **Marion Ladewig** was born in Grand Rapids, Michigan. At the age of 35 she began her dominance of women's bowling. She was the first to win the Bowling Proprietors' Association of America Woman's All-Star (now called the Women's US Open) title in 1949.

In the 1950 season, she won all-events titles on the city, state and national levels — becoming the only bowler in history to achieve this spectacular feat.

Between 1949 and 1963, she won the Women's US Open nine times; in 1951, her eight-day average was an amazing 247.5. She won the World Invitational in 1957, 1960, 1962, 1963 and 1964, and was the All Events champion of the Women's International Bowling Congress in 1950 and 1955.

The Bowling Writers Association named her Woman Bowler of the Year nine times in 1950-1954; 1957-1959; and in 1963. She was inducted into the Woman's International Bowling Congress Hall of Fame in 1963.

The Associated Press' 1963 Woman Athlete of the Year poll placed Ladewig third after golfer Mickey Wright and tennis champ Maria Bueno. This was the first time that a bowler had made it even close to the top.

She wrote syndicated columns, consulted on sportswear design and was an adviser to the Brunswick Corporation. Marion Ladewig retired from competition in 1965. She was a grandmother who had dominated her sport for almost 20 years: her career average was 190.

Marion Ladewig

Three-time Associated Press Female Athlete of the Year (1938, 1943 and 1945), winner of 15 major tournaments and 57 overall pro career wins, **Patricia Jane Berg** was born on February 13, 1918 in Minneapolis, Minnesota.

Always fond of sports, her parents channeled her energy and talent into golf when she was fourteen. They bought her a membership in the Interlachen Country Club. Within a year, she qualified for the Minnesota State Championships.

She won the National Amateur Tournament by age 20, and was already considered to be the best woman golfer in the US. Before becoming a pro, she played on the Curtis Cup team twice, and in her lifetime had 83 tournament victories.

Berg turned pro in 1940. She went on to win the first national Open in 1946; the Women's Masters (Titleholders Tournament) seven times; the Vare Trophy for lowest annual average three times; and the World Championship at Tam O'Shanter four times.

She was one of the founders of the Ladies Professional Golf Association, and served as its president from 1948-52. In 1952, she shot an astounding 64 in the Richmond Open — this stood as the LPGA 18-hole record for 12 years. She was the leading money winner of the LPGA three times.

Another point of excellence was that she had qualified for every tournament she had ever entered — a record she still holds. In 1951, she enterd the LPGA Hall of Fame, and continued to play championship-level golf into the 1970s.

Patty Berg

Like **Ty Cobb (see no. 17)**, his competitive instinct also had a crusty edge. As a rookie, it made life hard for him. **Theodore Samuel "Ted" Williams** had joined the San Diego Padres of the Pacific Coast League in 1935, hitting .291 in his second year. In 1938, the Boston Red Sox traded for Ted, but the usual needling dealt out to rookies by older players affected his performance: at the plate, he was distracted by thinking too much about the insults, and not enough about the ball.

He was sent down to a Boston farm team in Minneapolis, where he led the Triple-A Association with a .366 average, 142 RBIs and 42 home runs.

He went back to the Red Sox in 1939, deciding he would ignore the insults and concentrate on batting. His famous quote, "Hitting a baseball is the single most difficult thing to do in sport," was his guiding maxim for the rest of his career.

In later years, he penned a book, *The Science of Hitting*, considered to be the most cogent tome on the connecting of baseball bats with baseballs. He insisted that a good batter should have more walks than strikeouts: wait for the good ball, know the pitcher and what he pitches, and get the bat around quickly, moving your hips before moving your hands.

He was a pitcher's nightmare: he had an uncanny ability to tell balls from strikes, and led the league on getting to base on balls six consecutive times.

He played right field, and became the last player to bat .400 over a season, in 1941, with a .406 average (the first player with so high an average since 1930): He began the last doubleheader of that season at .399, and went six for eight to bring his average up to .406. He was also the youngest player to exceed .400.

He led the American League in batting six times; he won the Triple Crown (lead-

Ted Williams

ing the league in batting average, home runs and RBIs) in 1942 and 1947; he was Most Valuable Player in 1946 and 1949; and had a 19-year career batting average of .344 with 521 home runs. This was especially impressive in that Williams' career was interrupted twice — by service as a Marine Corps pilot in World War II and in the Korean War.

He was tall and slender, which combined with his skills to earn him his nickname, "The Splendid Splinter." As late as 1957, he led the league with a .388 batting average at the age of 39. He retired in 1960, with an average of .316. His last hit was a home run.

39. JACKIE ROBINSON
1919-1972 (Baseball Player)

He is remembered not only as a great athlete, but for breaking the color barrier in baseball, opening the major leagues to men of all races.

John Roosevelt "Jackie" Robinson was born in Cairo, Georgia, on January 31, 1919, but his mother moved the family to Pasadena, Californa shortly afterward when his father deserted them. Jackie grew up to attend UCLA, playing in four competitive sports, and achieving fame as a football player.

After college, he joined the army and was commissioned a Second Lieutenant. After this service, he signed on as a shortstop with the Kansas City Monarchs of the Negro National League.

Pee Wee Reese said of Robinson, his teammate for a decade, "When the chips were down, he was at his best." He was outspoken and candid, and his reaction to the difficulty of his position as the first black man to enter the white major leagues

Jackie Robinson

was grit and sometimes defiance. Brooklyn Dodgers owner Branch Rickey signed him on, and he began playing with the Dodgers in 1947. He was Rookie of the Year that same season; and Most Valuable Player of the National League in 1949. He played for the Dodgers until 1956, when he was traded to the New York Giants, and simultaneously announced his retirement.

He became an executive with the Choc Full o' Nuts restaurant chain, moving on to other executive positions in insurance, food franchising and construction. He was also active in the Republican party, serving as special assistant for community affairs under Nelson Rockefeller until the late 1960s.

As a baseball player, he was known for doing the seemingly impossible. One example of this was in the 1951 pennant race between the Dodgers and the Giants. It all came down to one game in September, a dark afternoon that got darker and darker. The rules stated that you could not turn on the lights for a game begun as early as two o'clock. The Dodgers had to win this one against the Philadelphia Phillies to pull even with the Giants and get back in the race.

It was the last day of the season, and a tie game in its thirteenth inning. With two out and the bases full of Phillies, batter Eddie Waitkus hit a fast line drive past second base, impossible to see in the darkening day. Suddenly, Robinson had it in his glove, flying with his body parallel to the flight of the ball.

The next inning, Pee Wee Reese popped up, as did Duke Snyder. Robinson took a ball and a strike, and then blew the next pitch out of the park for the win, setting up a pennant playoff with the Giants.

Jackie Robinson died in his home in Stamford, Connecticut on October 24, 1972.

46

40. JOHN DAVIS
1921-1984 (Weightlifter)

In addition to being the first African-American man to win the World Amateur Heavyweight Weightlifting Championship (in Paris, 1946), and the first black man to win an Olympic weightlifting championship, **John Davis** has the distinction of being one of the most dominant weightlifters of modern times. He was born in Brooklyn, New York on January 12, 1921. At 17, he competed as a Light Heavyweight in the 1938 World Championships in Vienna. He was undefeated in all competitions between 1938 and his retirement in 1953.

He was the World Champion at his weight classification six times, and won Gold Medals at two consecutive **Olympic Games** (1948 and 1952). From 1948-1956, he was the winner of 32 state, national, Olympic and World Weightlifting championships. He was the World's Amateur Heavyweight Champion in 1946, 1947, 1949, 1950 and 1951.

Davis outperformed his rivals in both Olympic competitions he entered in the press, the snatch and the jerk. In London, in 1948, he lifted 137.5 kg in the press and the snatch and 177.5 in the jerk; for a total of 452.5 kg. Norbert Schemansky won the silver that year.

In 1952, in Helsinki, Davis lifted 150 kg in the press, 145 kg in the snatch and 165 in the jerk for a total of 460 kg, winning the Gold Medal over James Bradford, who won the silver.

Athletics analyst David Willoughby postulates that Davis was a contender for the unofficial title of "The Greatest Middle-Heavyweight (90 kilos and under) Olympic Lifter on Record."

In 1941 (before "Middle-Heavyweight" became an officially recognized weight class), Davis completed lifts of 322.25 pounds in the press; 317.5 pounds in the snatch; and a clean and jerk of 370

John Davis

pounds, for a total of 1009.75 pounds. He was to go on to be a full-fledged Heavyweight. His best individual lifts were: 342 pounds in the press; snatch, 330.5 pounds; clean and jerk, 402 pounds. He could curl 215 pounds and bench press 425. He did a two-handed dead lift of 705 pounds.

John Davis, in addition to being a great weightlifting champion, blazed a path for others of his race.

41. ROCKY MARCIANO
1923-1969 (Boxer)

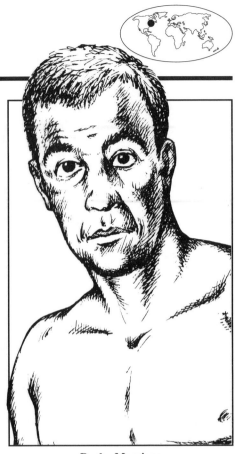

Rocky Marciano

His professional boxing record was 49 wins, and no losses. He fought the best fighters of all styles, and won. Ironically, at five feet 11 inches and 185 pounds, he was one of the smallest heavyweight champs, with a very short 68-inch reach.

He was a family man, known for his compassion. Yet, he fought with total focus, relentlessly. With a right or left, he could knock you out. When he beat **Joe Louis (see no. 35)** on October 26, 1951, Louis recalled, "I think it hurt him more than it did me ... he sent a message, saying how sorry he was the fight turned out the way it did."

On 30 December 1949, he sent Carmine Vingo to the hospital in the sixth round. When Vingo was left paralyzed from the waist down, Marciano paid the then-large sum of $2000 for his hospital bills.

He was born in Brockton, Massachusetts on September 1, 1923, christened **Rocco Francis Marchegiano**. When he joined the Army, he won his first "boxing match" (against the camp bully) in two rounds. Upon discharge, he became an amateur, losing just one match in his amateur career.

In his first pro bout, he knocked out (KO'd) Lee Epperson in three rounds on March 17, 1947. Then he signed with manager Al Weill, who, with trainer Charley Goldman, turned Marciano from a brawler into a boxer.

Marciano faced the sophisticated, technically superb Jersey Joe Walcott for the championship on September 23, 1952. For two full rounds of the fight, Rocky was blinded by medication that had been put on one of his facial cuts, but KO'd Walcott in the 13th round.

He defended his title six times — he KO'd Walcott in the first round in their return match; KO'd Roland Estarza in 11; outpointed Ezzard Charles in 15; KO'd Charles in eight on their return match;

KO'd Don Cockell in nine; and KO'd Archie Moore in nine.

The Moore fight was his last fight: on April 27, 1956, Marciano retired. His Spartan training regimen and public appearances disrupted his family life. His wife, Barbara, his mother, Pasqualina and his baby daughter required his presence.

He invested in bowling alleys, real estate, a construction company and other fighters. In 1969, he participated in a series of fight sequences with **Muhammad Ali (see no. 64)**, to be fed into a computer that would decide who was the best heavyweight of all. Marciano "won" by a "knockout" in the 13th round.

On August 31, 1969, he was killed in an airplane crash, while flying home to a birthday party hosted by his wife, daughter and 17-month-old son.

Born on June 18, 1924, in Joliet, Illinois, he would grow up to have an outstanding career, so much so that he would be selected by a 1950 Associated Press poll as the Greatest Basketball Player of the First Half of the Century. At six feet, 10 inches, he was the first of the really talented "big men" in post-World War II basketball.

George Mikan went to law school at De Paul University in Chicago, where he was also an outstanding basketball player. He went from there to a stint with the professional National Basketball League (NBL) team, the Chicago American Gears.

Early on in his career with the Gears, Mikan signed on as a Center with the Minneapolis Lakers. He would play with the Lakers for nine seasons, retiring in 1956, and coming back to coach for the 1957-58 season. Over that period, the Lakers would change leagues from the NBL to the Basketball Association of America to the National Basketball Association (NBA).

When the American Basketball Association was founded on February 2, 1967, Mikan was made its first commissioner. In 1969, the decision was made to move the ABA's offices from Minneapolis to New York, and Mikan resigned, in order to continue his successful law practice in Minneapolis.

In his career, Mikan averaged 20+ points per game and was named to the All-Star team for six consecutive seasons; played on the 1945 National Intercollegiate Tournament championship team with De Paul; played on five Minneapolis championship teams in six years, from 1949-54; was an all-American three times; and led the league in scoring three times, and rebounding once.

While he was with the Minneapolis Lakers, Mikan scored 11,764 points over nine regular seasons, for an average of 21.6 points per game; and 2141 points in 91 post-season games for a 23.5-point average in championship games.

George Mikan

43. DON CARTER
b. 1926 (Bowler)

He was voted the Greatest Bowler of All Time in 1970. He won the Professional Bowlers Association of America All-Star Tournament four times, in 1953, 1954, 1957, 1958. He won the first PBAA Championship in 1960, and he was voted Bowler of the Year six times, in 1953-54, 1957-58, 1960 and 1962.

In the PBAA All-Star (also known as the PBAA United States Open), Peterson scoring was used from 1942 through 1962. This meant that individual game winners got one point per game won, and an additional point for each fifty pins knocked down.

Carter's scores in the PBAA games were as follows: 1953 — 304.17 versus 297.36 for runner up Ed Lubanski; 1954 — 308.02 versus 307.25 for runner-up Bill Lillard (Lillard would win against Joe Wilman in 1956); 1957 — 308.49 versus 305.45 for runner-up Dick Weber (Weber would go on to become only the second bowler [after Carter] to win four championships in the tournament in 1962, 1963, 1965 and 1966); 1958 — 311.03 versus 308.09 for runner-up Buzz Fazio.

The Professional Bowlers Association of America was formed in 1958, and Carter's score in the first PBAA National Championship of 1960 was 6512 for 30 games. His win in the ABC Masters Tournament of 1961 was 211.18, downing runner-up Dick Hoover.

He was voted PBAA Bowler of the Year in 1953, 1954, 1957, 1958, 1960 and 1962. Carter led the PBAA tour in earnings as late in his career as 1962, with $22,525; and 1964 with $49, 972. He also led the PBAA in overall average, 212.84 for 1962.

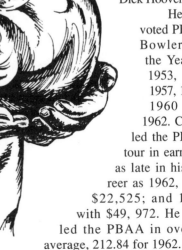

Don Carter

44. BOB COUSY
b. 1928 (Basketball Player)

Bob Cousy

Robert Joseph "Bob" Cousy was known for his phenomenal playmaking, which revolutionized the game of basketball. Born the son of French immigrants in New York City on August 9, 1928, Cousy spoke only French until he was six years old.

The family moved to St. Albans, Queens when he was 12, and in his junior high school years, he began his experiments with ball-handling — behind-the-back passes and other sleight of hand that would fool the opposition and help his own team to win. He didn't make the junior varsity squad at Andrew Jackson High School until his sophomore year; and in his junior year, he wasn't allowed to play until January, but in his senior year, he led the city in scoring and was named to the All-City team.

He went to Holy Cross College on a basketball scolarship, where, in his junior and senior years, he led the Crusaders to 26 straight wins and two phenomenal seasons. His ball handling influenced the entire starting five, and he was nicknamed "The Houdini of the Hardwood."

The Boston Celtics' new coach, Red Auerbach had a chance to draft him for the 1950-51 season, but chose a taller player, expressing the idea that he needed a taller man to help bring the last-place Celtics into contention. Cousy was picked by the Tri-Cities Blackhawks, and then was traded before the start of the season to the Chicago Stags, who promptly went defunct.

His name was put into a hat with two other Stags players, league-leading scorer Max Zaslosky and ace playmaker Andy Phillip. The Celtics, the Knicks and the Warriors had the pick: the Celtics got Cousy. Years later, Auerbach said, "We got stuck with the greatest player in the league when we drew his name out of a hat."

Cousy averaged 15.6 points a game to rocket the Celtics into second place in the East. In 1952, Chuck Share and Bill Sharman came on board as Auerbach continued to build his team around Cousy's ball handling. The team was now a solid contender.

In a 1953 Eastern Division playoff game against the Syracuse Nats, Cousy made 10 field goals and a playoff record 30 of 32 free throws, and 50 points overall. In the midst of the 1956-57 season, the team acquired **Bill Russell (see no. 51)**. Russell, with his defensive genius, and Cousy, with his brilliant playmaking, led the Celtics to championships in 1957, and 1959 through 1963.

Cousy himself led the league in assists eight times, and was chosen 10 times for the All-NBA first team. Cousy retired at 34 in 1963, leaving Sam Jones and KC Jones to carry the team with the ball-handling they had learned from him. He had revolutionized the game. Years later, after the Celtics ran up a record 11 NBA championship wins (eight of them in a row), Bill Russell said, "The image of the Celtics is the image of Bob Cousy."

45. GORDIE HOWE
b. 1928 (Hockey Player)

Gordie Howe

His nickname says it all: "Mr. Hockey." Until **Wayne Gretzky's (see no. 94)** breakthrough in 1994, **Gordie Howe** was the all-time National Hockey League leader in goals scored with 801; once led the league in scoring with 1850 points; played a record 32 seasons with the NHL and the World Hockey League; was on the all-NHL first team 12 times; was Most Valuable Player in the NHL six times (1952, 1953, 1957, 1958, 1960 and 1963) and in the WHL once; and led the NHL in scoring six times. He also set an NHL record for assists.

He was born on March 31, 1928 in Floral, Saskatchewan. The family soon moved to nearby Saskatoon, where Gordie learned to play hockey. Every school and playground had a skating rink, and the Howes had one in their back yard. Gordie played in boyhood games with improvised equipment (second-hand skates, shinboards made from magazines and rubber bands, and a tennis-ball puck!).

By the time he was 15, the NHL wanted him, but Gordie turned homesick at the New York Rangers camp in Winnipeg. The next year, the Detroit Red Wings signed him to a contract. He was 16, too young to play pro hockey, so he went down to a farm team for exhibitions, and came back up to the Red Wings at age 18.

His first three years with Detroit were unspectacular, but he made a name in the 1949 Stanley Cup competition, with eight goals and three assists, unmatched by any other player that year. The next year, he suffered a fractured skull in the playoffs, when he was (it was rumored) fouled and sent crashing into the sideboards.

He recovered to lead the league in scoring in 1951, 1952, 1953 and 1954. He was the only player of his time who could shoot and stick-handle right- or left-handed.

On his 25th anniversary with the Red Wings, NHL coaches named him "The smartest player, best passer, best playmaker and best puck carrier" in the league. His sons Mark and Marty were by then also playing for the Red Wings.

Ironically, the Red Wings took him off the ice and put him in a front-office job. Shortly after, Howe and his sons departed for the Houston Aeros of the World Hockey Association. He led the Aeros to the championship in 1972 and he was also chosen to play for Team Canada against the Soviet Union's All-Star team that year. Team Canada won, 4-3-1.

Gordie returned to win the WHA's MVP Award in 1974, and led the Aeros to another championship in 1975. Howe and sons signed with the WHA's Hartford Whalers in 1977. The Whalers joined the NHL in 1979, and were the only former WHA team to earn a playoff spot that year, which the Whalers attributed to the 50-year-old Howe's playing and leadership. Howe retired at the age of 51, having become a legend in his own time.

The phenomenon of **Arnold Daniel Palmer** came along just in time to show the masses of television-watching sports fans that golf could produce an interesting personality: a champion who was also personable; a master of his sport who also brought drama to the course by valor and an ability to work miracles of play.

Of course, he was a consummate golfer. In 1960, he was 14th going into the final round at the US Open. He birdied six of the first seven holes, scored a US Open record-matching 30 for the first nine holes, and finished the second nine in 35, for a 65, the lowest final round ever shot by a US Open winner to his time. His total for the four rounds was 280, two strokes ahead of the then-amateur **Jack Nicklaus (see no. 60)**.

He was born in Latrobe, Pennsylvania, where his father was a greenskeeper and club professional at the local golf course. He became a caddie at the course when he was 11. In 1946, he entered his first national contest, a juniors tournament.

He joined the Coast Guard when his best friend was killed in an auto accident, and when he was discharged, he became a sales representative. But he continued playing golf, and in 1954 he won the National Amateur Championship and he became a pro. He and his new wife Winnie scraped and scrambled to survive, but the money would come. In 1958, he led the PGA with $42,607 in winnings.

He set a single-season record of over $125,000 in 1963, and his business interests — a company that manufactured golf clubs and clothing; a chain of putting courses; his own writing, teaching and appearances in the media — made him even more. His personal income was over $1 million per year, but his golf started to suffer. He had numerous slumps in the late 1960s.

He rallied — 1971 was a landmark year.

He won four big tournaments that year; his earnings went past the $200,000 mark, and he was named "Athlete of the Decade." Arnold Palmer continues to be one of the most-listened-to and august voices of the game of golf.

Palmer had 60 pro career wins and was the first golfer to exceed $1 million in career earnings. He won the Masters at Augusta in 1958, 1960, 1962 and 1964. He won the British Open in 1961 and 1962. He was PGA Player of the Year in 1960 and 1962. In 1954, he won the US Amateur championship; he won the US Open in 1960. On the Seniors tour, by 1994, he had 10 career wins; including two Championships in 1980 and 1984; and one Senior US Open in 1981.

He has often been a spokesman for the game, and for two decades was golfing's most recognizable player, thanks to his warmth and dramatic personality. His following was so large that he patented the name for them: "Arnie's Army." Fans felt that they shared every moment of tension, relief, disappointment and triumph with him. Rugged-looking, slender Arnold Palmer was "easy to read" on the course.

Arnold Palmer

47. JACQUES PLANTE
1929 - 1986 (Hockey Player)

Jacques Plante was the greatest of all hockey goaltenders — he changed the game substantially in that he considerably upped the ante for all goalies to follow, and also provided a useful safety example in that he was the first goalie to wear a mask as a regular piece of equipment.

In his 20-year career, he played for Montreal, New York, Seattle, Toronto and Boston. Most of his career was played for Montreal from 1952 to 1962.

Goaltenders don't get the media attention that high scorers on the offense do, but they are equal in importance. The goalie has to keep the puck out of the goal, and in many cases bears the burden of a losing game.

Also, goalies have to contend with high-speed assault via hard-rubber pucks. In the days when goalies wore no masks, their faces were ribboned with scars after their first full season; it was a rare case when a goalie had not suffered multiple fractures of all facial bones in his career.

He was Goaltender of the Year an all-time record seven times, in 1955, 1956, 1957, 1958, 1959, 1961 and 1968; and led Montreal to Stanley Cup championships in 1953, 1956, 1957, 1958, 1959 and 1960. He also won the Most Valuable Player award in 1961. He is second all-time in wins, with 434 to his credit. Plante is also second in goals against average amongst modern players, at 2.38, leading the league in this category eight times.

His outstanding presence and abilities as a goaltender gave courage and spirit to his teams. Plante's name is practically synonymous with the position he played.

Plante's mask was a move in the direction of common sense and humanitarian concern for the one player on the team who was always on the receiving end of the ever-furious action in a hockey game. Goaltending was, and remains, a highly dangerous occupation, demanding extraordinary reflexes, nerves of steel and constant vigilance.

Jacques Plante is remembered as a man who did substantial benefit for the game of hockey, raising standards in all facets of his endeavor.

Jacques Plante

48. ROGER BANNISTER
b. 1929 (Runner)

For hundreds of years, it was deemed to be impossible to break one of mankind's great barriers — the four-minute mile. **Paavo Nurmi (see no. 24)** set a mile record of 4:10.4 in 1922, and his was followed in 1945 by Gunder Haegg's run, lowering the time to an amazing 4:01.4.

In 1952, Australian runner John Landy made it known that the four-minute mile was his goal, and he proceeded to run 4:02.1, followed by 4:02.6. At the same time, English medical student and Olympic-class runner **Roger Gilbert Bannister** was studying Landy's runs. Bannister persevered in his belief that, like Nurmi, he could better his own time substantially by intensive training, combined with a careful analysis of running conditions, pacing, timed acceleration and other factors that could be built into a "game plan" for a given race.

Bannister knew he would have to run four laps at the lowest speed possible to attain the four-minute mile: four laps averaging 60 seconds each. In May 1953, he put his plan to the test, but ran the first two laps too slowly. Still, he achieved a new British mile record of 4:03.6.

Meanwhile, in December of that year, Landy ran his best ever, a mile in 4:02 — but his subsequent attempts did no better. Significantly, Landy said he felt the barrier was "a brick wall."

That meant Bannister would *have* to be the pioneer. Bannister stepped up his training from December 1953 through the Spring of 1954. He knew the race in which he would go for the record would be a match between the Oxford University team and the British Amateur Athletic Association team. Bannister would run for the BAAA, on May 6, 1954. He stopped training a few days before, to conserve his energy for the race.

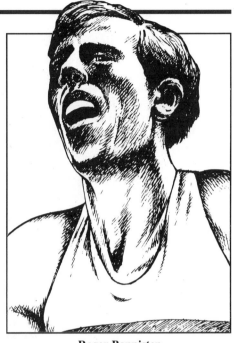

Roger Bannister

Bannister lined up with the others that day, the gun went off, and he ran the first quarter in 57.5 seconds; at the half-mile, he was running 1:58; his three-quarters time was 3:00.5; and he broke the tape at 3:59.4 — a new world record, and a seemingly immovable barrier surmounted.

Just over a month later, Landy clocked 3:58. That set the stage for a match between Bannister and Landy — at Empire Stadium, in Vancouver, British Columbia, on June 21, 1954, a featured event at the British Commonwealth Games.

Landy led through three laps, with Bannister gradually catching up to pass him in the fourth lap stretch, for the win at 3:58.8. Bannister went on to receive his medical degree in July of that year. His last win in international competition was in the 1500-meter race in the European games later that year; he then announced his retirement from running.

Patricia McCormick is the only woman diver to win two Gold Medals in two consecutive Olympics, both times for platform diving and springboard diving, in 1952 and 1956.

She was born near Seal Beach, California, and quickly took to the water, winning her first diving trophy, the Long Beach One-Meter Gold Cup, at the age of 14.

Her training was rigorous, and she often used complex, dangerous dives to prepare herself for the regimen and accuracy necessary to win major competitions, where such dives were not allowed: a way of fine-tuning herself by demanding more from herself than she would actually need.

As of 1951, she was the US Champion. In 1950 she had become the first woman to sweep all the Amateur Athletic Union outdoor diving titles. In 1952, she won all the AAU indoor titles, too.

Pat McCormick

In her first Olympics at Helsinki, Finland, she won her first two Olympic Golds. She followed suit in the next Olympics, in Melbourne, Australia, in 1956. That same year, she won the Sullivan Award as the Number One Amateur Athlete in the US.

Pat's Olympics regimen included a two-and-one-half hour drill on the 33-foot high platform; then two hours of springboard practice daily, plus an evening three-hour workout, for 80 to 100 dives per day, six days per week.

That diving is a dangerous sport was attested to by the various scars, cracked ribs, lacerations, broken fingers and other injuries she sustained over her career. In a sport that demands absolute concentration, great courage, and almost supernatural grace, Pat McCormick was known as the best diver in the world during her tenure, and set new marks for others to follow.

Only she and the much later **Greg Louganis (see no. 89)** had triumphed over the intense Olympic diving competition to prevail twice in two consecutive Olympics.

At four feet eleven and approximately 103 pounds, **William Lee "Willie" Shoemaker** is one of the towering sports figures of our century. He possesses the world record for horseracing wins at 8833. Shoemaker won the Belmont Stakes in 1957, 1959, 1962, 1967 and 1975; the Kentucky Derby in 1955, 1959, 1965, 1986 (at age 54, he was the oldest rider to win this one); the Preakness in 1963 and 1967; and won the Eclipse Award in 1981, with special awards going to him in 1976 and 1981.

If **Gordie Howe (see no 45)** is "Mr. Hockey," Shoemaker is "Mr. Horseracing." In the 1960s and 1970s, he was king of his world. With more than 560 stakes wins by 1972, he held the record in stakes wins with more than 554; he also held the record in wins with added money of $100,000 or more. He was far above everyone else in money earned by his mounts, and he himself earned more than $5 million in the first quarter century of his career — and that figure has understandably risen since.

He was born on a cotton farm near Fabens, Texas. A premature baby, he weighed two-and-one-half pounds. His grandmother nutured him in a shoebox placed on the door of a warm oven, and Bill survived against the doctor's predictions.

He weighed 85 pounds in high school, with tremendous wiry strength for his size. He once won a boxing competition against boys of 100 pounds and more.

He became interested in horseracing around that time, theorizing that "Around the race track, I'd only have to compete against guys my own size." He worked as a groom and exercise boy at a ranch, saving enough money to go to California and catch on as an exercise rider. Trainer George Reeves saw Bill and was impressed enough to get him his first race.

Bill won his third race — auspiciously early in his career for a rookie jockey — on a horse he always has said "was a lot smarter than I was." His first year, he won 219 times; the second year, with 388 wins, he tied for the jockey title; the third year he set an all-time record of 485 wins.

The legend of Willie Shoemaker had begun. Part of that legend was that he was actually a nice guy — in the mornings, even after winning an important race, he'd be down at the paddock, exercising horses and bantering with the exercise riders who, for some jockeys, were beneath notice.

His style was characterized by a smooth, rhythmic style, with no wasted motion on the part of him or the horse. He used the whip sparingly, and often hung back at the beginning of a race, waiting till the others had made their moves before he passed them and won the race. He studied each horse's history, its wins and losses, trying to discern the motivations behind peak performances. He would use what he learned when he mounted the horse, often getting suprising performance out of underrated horses.

The great horses he rode included Swaps, Ack Ack, Gallant Man, Coaltown, Tomy Lee, Silky Sullivan, Sword Dancer, Jaipur, Candy Spots, Never Bend, Gun Bow, Northern Dancer, Tom Rolfe, Buck Passer, Damascus and more on a list that reads like a "who's who" of horses.

Shoemaker retired from competitive riding in 1990 to become a horse trainer. In 1991, he suffered an auto accident that paralyzed him from the neck down, but he continues to direct the training of horses.

51. BILL RUSSELL
b. 1934 (Basketball Player)

Bill Russell

William Felton Russell was born on February 12, 1934, in Monroe, Louisiana, but would grow up in Oakland, California, where as he grew older, his height increased disproportionally. He failed to make his junior high basketball team, and barely made the high school team.

He had an undistinguished high school career but a coach from the University of San Francisco saw something in him that was scholarship material. USF was a basketball unknown at the time, but Russell and teammate KC Jones (also a Celtic teammate in later years) turned them into a powerhouse, posting 55 consecutve wins at one point, from 1954-56, making USF the NCAA Champion and the nation's top-rated college team.

Russell was also the number one college player. He turned down an offer to go pro upon graduation, opting to play with the US team in the 1956 Olympics, instead. The US team won the Gold. Then, Russell was grabbed by Red Auerbach's Celtics. With Cousy's speeded-up playmaking, they needed a tall man who could get them the ball. Russell was that man. Russell's contract was a new high salary for a rookie at the time: $24,000. Auerbach knew what he had, Russell knew what to do, and the rest is history.

Bill Russell added the necessary extra ingredient to the game of basketball, after **Bob Cousy (see no. 44)** had added his leaven of spectacular play-making. Russell's was shot blocking and intensive rebounding. Previous to Russell, basketball centers were the guys who stuffed the basketball into the hoop.

Russell's technique was to take this function to the other end of the court, and stuff the ball *down the other team's throats*. Then again, the center gets the rebound, too. Much more than just a good scorer, the center's main functions in the contempo-

rary game are to block the opposition's shots and to feed the ball to his team. Russell is responsible for working that transformation. He was also the first black man to coach an NBA team.

That he and Cousy should happen to the same team in an overlapping time frame was what made the Boston Celtics the most dominant team in basketball history. In 13 seasons with the Celtics, Russell led the team to 11 NBA championships, in 1957, 1959, 1960, 1961, 1962, 1963, 1964, 1965,1966, 1968 and 1969.

He won the Most Valuable Player Award five times; had 21,620 career rebounds, with a rebounding average of 22.5; set a record of rebounds per game, at 51; and led the league in rebounding four times.

Russell coached the Celtics from 1966-1968, winning an NBA Championshp in 1968. He retired the following year to become a sportscaster. He returned to basketball in 1973 to coach the Seattle Supersonics. In 1974, Russell was elected to the Hall of Fame, and in 1975, the Supersonics made the playoffs for the first time.

52. HENRY AARON
b. 1934 (Baseball Player)

Henry Aaron made the statement, "records are made to be broken," and proceeded to break a few, as the all-time leader in home runs, with 755, and runs-batted-in, with 2297. Also, he is the all-time third in hits, with 3771. He won a Most Valuable Player Award in 1957; led the National League in home runs and RBIs four times each; led in runs scored three times; also led the league in hits and batting average twice (1956, .328; and 1959, .355). He had 44 homers four times.

In 1972, he became the highest-paid baseball player to that time with a three-year contract averaging $200,000 per year.

Henry Aaron was born in a district of Mobile, Alabama whose high school had no baseball team. He came up to adulthood playing in sandlot teams, and signed on with the Indianapolis Clowns at the age of 17. By year's end, his contract was picked up by the Atlanta Braves. His first season with a Braves farm team, he was voted Rookie of the Year in the Northern League; his second saw him winning Most Valuable Player in the South Atlantic League, for a Jacksonville team, where he played shortstop. The Braves had him shifted to outfield for a stint in the Puerto Rican League with the team Caguas. He hit .324 for Caguas, tied for the home run title, and had second in RBIs. Caguas won the Caribbean World Series that year.

The Braves finally invited him to big-league spring training in 1954. Aaron showed he could line drive to all points of play. He played respectably in 122 games that first year, with a .280 batting average, 13 homers and 69 RBIs. The second year got better, with 27 homers, 26 RBIs and a .314 batting average.

He was always dependable as an outfielder, often catching balls that were considered too high or too fast by other fielders. He had home run totals of 44, 30, 39,

Henry Aaron

40, 34, 45 and 44 through the latter 1950s and early 1960s, and was hitting well in the three hundreds, so well that opposing pitchers often felt Aaron psyched them out by "knowing" what they would pitch next. He will be most remembered for eclipsing **Babe Ruth**'s **(see no. 21)** home run record of 714 on April 8, 1974, and for setting his own mark of 755. Hank Aaron retired in 1976, and his jersey number, 44, was retired by the two major league teams with whom he played for over 22 years, Atlanta and Milwaukee. He was named to the Hall of Fame in 1982.

Larissa Latynina won a total of 18 medals (including five silver and four bronze) over three Olympics in 1956, 1960 and 1964 — making her the all-time, overall leading Olympic medal winner. She is also the only woman gymnast to win nine Olympic Gold medals, rounding out her record as the most prolific Olympic medal winner of modern times.

She was born on December 27, 1934 in Khorson, Ukraine. Her abilities became apparent early, and she went on to formal education at the Kiev State Institute of Physical Culture.

She won the individual All-Around Olympic Championship in 1956 and 1960, with scores of 74.933 and 77.031, respectively. She won the vault in 1966 with 18.833 points.

In 1956, she tied with Agnes Keleti of Hungary in the floor exercise, with 18.733 points. She won the floor exercise in three consecutive Olympics — 1956 (tied for first), 1960 and 1964, with 18.733, 19.583 and 19.599 points, respectively.

Her team won the Team Combined Olympics Gymnastics competition in 1956, 1960 and 1964 with 444.80, 382.320 and 280.890 points, respectively.

In addition to this, she was the All-Around World Champion in 1958 and 1962; Word Champion in the floor exercise in 1962; World Champion in the uneven bars in 1958; World Champion on the balance beam in 1958; and World Champion in the vault in 1958.

Laryssa Latynina established a path that such later gymnastics stars from the USSR as Olga Korbut would follow.

On retirement from competition, she became the national senior gymnastic coach, and helped plan for her country's outstanding gymnastic teams in future Olympics.

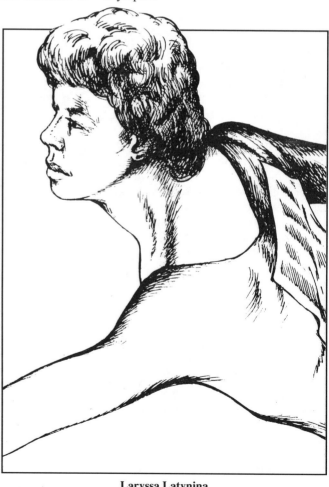

Laryssa Latynina

54. A.J. FOYT
b. 1935 (Auto Racer)

A.J. Foyt

Anthony Joseph "A.J." Foyt is one of the all-time greats of auto racing. His prolific racing career has produced wins in almost every field of racing endeavour, save the blunt, brutal acceleration of pro drag racing.

He is the all-time leader in Indy Car victories with 67; he won the Indianapolis 500 four times, in 1961, 1964, 1967 and 1977. Among the major races he has won are the 1972 Daytona 500 and the 24 Hours of Le Mans in 1967. He was the United States Auto Club (USAC) Champion a record seven times, in 1960, 1961, 1963, 1964, 1967, 1975 and 1979; and he won the 24 Hours of Daytona twice, in 1983 and 1985.

At home in any kind of racing car, he has been one of auto racing's most inspirational competitors. He is "Tex" to his friends, "A.J." to the media and just plain "Foyt!" to his competitors. He was born on January 16, 1935, the son of Anthony Joseph Foyt, Sr. A.J. Senior was a part-time race driver, but a full-time mechanical genius, who could tune every available foot-pound of horsepower from an engine.

A.J. won his first race against an adult at the age of five, in a car his father built. He would go on to win millions of dollars in prize money in a legendary career. In tenth grade, he threw himself full force into the world of racing — sprint cars, midgets, stock cars — anything he could get a ride in, and came to dominate most of the tracks where he raced.

He moved on to the midwest at 18, running against the big names of the early 1950s. He was already becoming known when he joined USAC, an advance preparation for eventually racing in the Indy 500. His first USAC event was a midget race in 1956; by 1958 his reputation was already such that he was invited to drive one of the legendary Dean Van Lines Specials in the Indy 500. He passed his Indy rookie test with ease, and placed 16th in the 500.

He rode with Dean again in 1959, placing 10th in the Indy 500, and drove for Dean the rest of the season, winning his first national driving championship that same year.

He is a hard man, gritty, unsparing in criticism at times. It served him well: the competition was always intense, and one's life was always on the line in the 150-to-180-mile-an-hour ranges in which he drove. He won his first Indy 500 in 1961, after a race-long duel with Eddy Sachs. They traded the lead several times, but Foyt ran out of fuel with 38 miles to go. He made a pit stop, refueled, and roared after Sachs.

Sach's tires were wearing, showing white cord; and, shades of **Tazio Nuvolari (see no. 19)**, Foyt passed him for the win when Sachs was forced to the pits for a tire change. Foyt would keep up the pace for the rest of his career, running on small tracks, or big circuits, stock cars or Indy Cars or Formula One, always a tough competitor whose name came into the common parlance in the same breath as the words "auto racing."

55. SANDY KOUFAX
b. 1935 (Baseball Player)

In a career spanning only 11 years, left-handed **Sanford "Sandy" Koufax** established one of the best records in baseball history. He was born on December 30, 1935, in Brooklyn, New York. At Lafayette High, he played first base and pitched for the baseball team, but his main sport was basketball. He went to the University of Cincinnati on a basketball scholarship.

The basketball coach talked him into playing baseball to keep in shape for basketball. Koufax was a lousy hitter at the time and decided he'd be more valuable as a pitcher than a first baseman, so he pitched. He pitched hard and fast, but with little control. A Brooklyn Dodgers scout saw him, and he eventually signed with the Dodgers in 1955 (the team would become the Los Angeles Dodgers in 1958).

His first five seasons were a struggle, and his win record was a mere 11 games in one season. In 1961, he was to get advice from Norm Sherry that would be invaluable. Sherry advised him to stop throwing hard each time; rather, to throw easy and simply get the ball over the plate. That advice resulted in a new technique for Koufax, and a whole new world of winning for him.

His record was 18-13 that season. The next season, he pitched his first no-hitter, against the Mets, and won 14 games by July, but a finger infection kept him out the rest of the season.

He came back strong the next season. On May 11, 1963, he pitched a no-hitter against the Giants, for an 8-0 score. His record that year was 25-5, and he won the Cy Young Award for best pitcher in the league. He had 306 strikeouts that year for a National League record.

The Dodgers won the pennant that year, and Koufax opened the Series for them against the Yankees. He was facing such Yankee batters as powerful sluggers **Mickey Mantle (b. 1931)** and **Roger**

Sandy Koufax

Maris (1934-1985); the opposing pitcher was the legendary **Whitey Ford (b. 1926)**. Koufax won the game 5-2 and established a new strikeout record, 15, for a World Series Game. He had truly arrived.

He was to retire in 1966, with persistent arthritic elbow trouble. But he established a towering record in the time he did play. He won the Cy Young Award in 1963, 1965 and 1966; he pitched one perfect game and three no-hitters. He was the league leader in Earned Run Average for five consecutive seasons; led the league in strikeouts four times; won over 25 games three times; and won the Most Valuable Player Award in 1963, and the World Series MVP Award in 1963 and 1965. His career record for 11 seasons was 165-87, with a 2.76 ERA.

There was a time when very tall men were expected to be uncordinated, clumsy and a detriment to any sporting endeavor. At seven feet, two inches in height, **Wilton Norman Chamberlain** proved that conception wrong. He became the most dominant basketball player of all time.

He would become a seven-time All-Star. He averaged over 50 points and over 40 points per game per season once each; over 30 and over 20 five times each. He led the league in scoring seven consecutive seasons, rebounding 11 seasons, field goals nine times, assists once and became Most Valuable Player in the playoffs in 1972.

He is the all-time leader in rebounds (55) and points scored in a single game (100). In 1960 he was Rookie of the Year. He had four overall Most Valuable Player awards — 1960, 1966, 1967 and 1968. He was the all-time leader in rebounds (23,924), and rebounding average per game (22.9); points per season (4029 in 1962); average points per game (50.4 in 1962); field goal percentage (.727 in 1973); and rebounding average (27.2). He was second in all-time most field goals made (12,681), as well as second all-time most points scored (31,419).

He was named College Player of the year in 1957, playing for the University of Kansas. He left at the end of his junior year in 1958, signing on for a barnstorming tour of basketball flash and dazzle with the Harlem Globetrotters, saying that he wanted to earn some money to help his poor parents out. In 1959, he signed on with the Philadelphia Warriors team (the 76ers didn't come into being until 1963).

Celtics coach Red Auerbach said, "He'll take over this league. The first time he meets **Bill Russell (see no. 51)**, we could fill Yankee Stadium." That dream came true, even though the venue was Boston Garden. Chamberlain finished with 30 points and 28 rebounds, while Russell had 22 points and 35 rebounds.

Russell, the master defense player, playing against Chamberlain, the spectacular rookie star, was the first player *ever* to block one of Wilt's shots. The Celtics won, 115-106.

On March 2, 1962, the Warriors played the New York Knicks in Hershey, Pennsylvania. The Warriors won, 169-147. Chamberlain had scored 100 of those points. The Knicks center Darrall Imhoff, assigned to guard Chamberlain, said "He was picking us up and stuffing us through the hoop with the ball," — and he was only slightly exaggerating.

Still, the Boston Celtics dominated the league; the Warriors failed to win a championship. In the 1963-64 season, Wilt was traded to the new franchise, the Philadelphia 76ers. In the 1966-67 season, the 76ers won the league championship, beating the Celtics and San Francisco. In 1968, he was traded to the Los Angeles Lakers, where he played on the winning team for another championship in 1972. He retired after the 1972-73 season.

Wilt Chamberlain

57. JIM BROWN
b. 1936 (Football Player)

In a career that was enacted in the days of the 12- and 14-game football seasons, fullback **James Nathaniel Brown** set a record of 126 career touchdowns that was only eclipsed in 1994 when Jerry Rice scored his 127th. He led the league in rushing eight times; was Player of the Year four times, 1957, 1958, 1963 and 1965. He rushed for over 1000 yards in each of seven seasons, over 200 yards per game in four games, and over 100 yards per game in 54 games. He was Rookie of the Year in 1957, and All-American at Syracuse. He never missed a game in his career, and played throughout his career for the Cleveland Browns.

He had enough power to knock tacklers down or drag them for a dozen yards, yet he was fast enough to outrun most defensive backs. It usually took two or more tacklers to bring him down. He ran close to

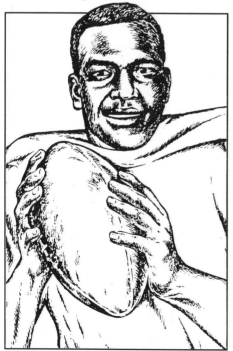

Jim Brown

the ground, in a gliding style.

He was born on February 17, 1936, on St. Simon's Island, Georgia. His mother moved to Manhasset, Long Island when he was two: he stayed with his grandparents, and eventually joined his mother when he was seven. He excelled in many sports in high school, earning a reputation as one of the best high school athletes in New York history.

He excelled at basketball, baseball, lacrosse and football. He had 42 scholarship offers when he graduated, yet he chose Syracuse, one of the few schools that offered him no scholarship. A friend of his, a local lawyer who wanted to see him succeed, pooled a group of Jim Brown fans and they paid his way to the University.

At Syracuse, he won 10 varsity letters, two apiece in track and baseball, and three apiece in lacrosse and football. He was All-American in lacrosse and football. In his last senior football game, he scored 43 points in a Syracuse 67-6 win over Colgate. In the Cotton Bowl that year, Brown rushed for 132 yards and scored 21 points.

The Cleveland Browns drafted him, and he started at fullback the first season. On November 24, 1957, Jim carried the ball 31 times for 237 yards and four touchdowns to help the Browns edge Los Angeles 45-21. In his first five years with the Browns, he gained 6463 yards on 1269 carries.

In 1963, Cleveland fired coach Paul Brown and hired Blanton Collier. That season, Brown became the first football running back to gain more than a mile in a season of play, averaging 133 yards per game for a total of 1863 yards. He retired in 1966 at the peak of his career, being hailed as the best running back of all time, to pursue an acting career. He was to star in over 20 motion pictures and dozens of television shows.

58. RICHARD PETTY
b. 1937 (Auto Racer)

Richard Petty

He was the first stock car driver to win $1 million in prize money, is the all-time NASCAR leader in wins, with 200; 127 pole positions, and 27 wins in a single season, 27 in 1967. He won the Daytona 500 seven times between 1964 and 1981, and was the NASCAR national driving champion in 1964, 1967, 1971, 1972, 1974, 1975 and 1979.

Richard Petty was born on July 2, 1937, the son of Lee Petty, a three-time Grand Nationals stock car champion with 54 career wins. Richard often indicated that he became a race car driver because his father was one, and he liked racing.

In 1959, Richard raced in the first Daytona 500 — a race his father won — but his own car broke down after 20 miles. However he did well enough in other races to become the NASCAR Rookie of the Year. He raced well for several years, but the family's informal sponsorship links to the Plymouth division of Chrysler Corporation was not helping them to win. Plymouth had yet to make a substantial commitment to racing, and hence the Petty cars were sometimes up against higher-horsepower competition.

Not only that, Lee was forced to go from the driver's seat to the pits because of injuries, and that left Richard alone to carry the family racing honors.

In 1964, Plymouth decided to fully, formally back Petty and another car owner, Ray Nichel, whose driver was Paul Goldsmith. Plymouth also invested in some serious horsepower for its teams: the new Chrysler 426 hemispherical combustion chamber engine, with high-end torque that was unbeatable, and would dominate the US racing scene for the next decade.

Goldsmith and Petty qualified at 174.9 and 174.4 mph, respectively. Richard Petty won the Daytona 500 that year, setting a world record of 154.3 mph, one lap ahead of the runner-up and 10 miles ahead of the third place finsher. In 1966, he won Daytona again. He would go on to become one of the legends of stock car racing, his famous chalk-blue "Number 43" Plymouths terrorizing the Ford factory teams of the 1960s and early 1970s.

In 1979, Richard Petty would become the first owner-driver to win the Winston Cup. In a long career that included not only driving cars but race-engineering them, Petty competitively banged bumpers with **A.J. Foyt (see no. 54)**, Bobby Allison, Junior Johnson, Fred Lorenzen, David Pearson, Lee Roy Yarbrough and a host of other top racing drivers.

59. ROD LAVER
b. 1938 (Tennis Player)

Probably the greatest tennis player in Australian history, **Rod Laver** is also the only player to win the Grand Slam (winning the Australian, British, French and US Opens in one year) *twice*. He did it as an amateur in 1962, and as a pro in 1969. He also won eight Grand Slam Doubles championships. He has 47 career tournament wins. His murderous backhand served him well in winning four Wimbledons, three Australian Championships, two French and two US championships.

He was rated Number One in 1961 and 1962, and then, when he became professional (pros weren't rated until 1968) he was considered number one from 1965 to 1967, when the ratings system caught up with the pros, and Laver was officially rated Number One in 1968 and 1969.

He was the first tennis player to earn $1 million in prize money, and played on the Australian Davis Cup team which was undefeated from 1959 to 1962. He shares the all-time Men's Grand Slam singles wins, 11, with Bjorn Borg.

He was proclaimed the world's greatest amateur tennis player in 1962, when he won his first Grand Slam, also winning the Italian, Netherlands, Norwegian and Swiss championships that same year. This was one of the greatest achievements in sports history.

For his first Grand Slam, he beat arch rival Roy Emerson in four sets for the Australian Open; beat Marty Mulligan in three at Wimbledon; beat Emerson again in five sets to take the French Open; and beat Emerson once again in the US Open, in four sets.

He lost 14 of his first 16 pro matches in 1963, but continued in the same style that had made him a great amateur: powerful volley strokes, and a unique, spinning serve that was hard to return effectively. By 1965, he was the number one pro in the world. His forehand and backhand were considered the best, ever.

When Wimbledon opened play to professionals in 1968, Laver became the first pro to win Wimbledon; he repeated in 1969, en route to his second career Grand Slam.

In the Australian, he beat Andres Gimeno 6-3, 6-4, 7-5 to win; in the French Open, he dropped Ken Rosewall 6-4, 6-3, 6-4 to win; at Wimbledon, he defeated John Newcombe 6-4, 5-7, 6-4, 6-4; and in the US Open, he won over Tony Roche, 7-9, 6-1, 6-2, 6-2.

He was rated in the Top 10 until 1975.

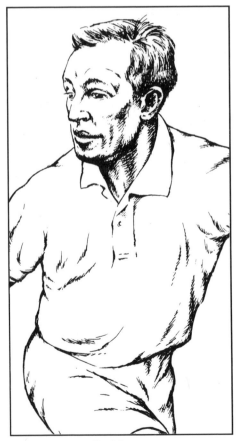

Rod Laver

60. JACK NICKLAUS
b. 1940 (Golfer)

Jack Nicklaus

Jack William Nicklaus has been called the greatest golfer of all time. The Professional Golf Association named him "Golfer of the Century" in 1988. He hits every shot as if it counts: his cool concentration during a game is unmatched. His putting is superb. Once, Tom Weiskopf asked him if he ever missed a long putt. He replied, "Not in my mind, I haven't."

He inherited a love of sports from his athletic father, Louis Nicklaus. He was born in Columbus, Ohio, on January 21, 1940, and after a youth of excelling in such sports as football, baseball, basketball and track, he concentrated on golf during his college years (1957-62) at Ohio State University.

His decision to concentrate on golf was made while playing on the US Walker Cup team in 1959. He won two of his matches and largely helped the US team to win. Unsure of his ability before that, he now understood his potential, and began to push himself harder.

He went on to capture the US Amateur Championship that same year, and came in second to legendary pro **Arnold Palmer (see no. 46)** in the 1960 US Open, where Jack's 282 for 72 holes was the best ever shot by an amateur to that date. He had planned to go into the insurance business, but in November 1961, opted to become a pro golfer instead. His first five months and 17 tournaments as a pro were devoid of a win — but he always finished in the money.

In June 1962, he tied Arnold Palmer in the US Open. Palmer was recognized as the overwhelming favorite, so the playoff had the aura of a legend in the making. Nicklaus won it, 71-74, becoming the youngest player to win the Open in golf history, and establishing a reputation that he would only build in the years to come.

He has won more than 90 tournament victories worldwide, including: National Collegiate Athletic Association Championship, 1961; the US Amateur in 1959 and 1961; the British Open, 1966, 1970 and 1978; the PGA Championship, 1963, 1971, 1973, 1975 and 1980; the World Open, 1976; the Australian Open, 1964, 1968, 1971, 1975, 1976 and 1978; plus six Masters and four US Opens.

A six-time Ryder Cup team member, he was captain of the US team in 1983 and 1987. His total of 70 PGA tour wins is second only to Sam Snead's awesome 81. In 1993, he won his second US Seniors Open. He has won 20 major championships — more than any other golfer. He astonished the golfing world when he won his sixth Masters at age 46 in 1986.

He has received the PGA Player of the Year Award for 1967, 1972, 1973, 1975 and 1976; the Byron Nelson Award for 1965, 1967 and 1972; the Dunlop Professional Athlete Award for 1972; *Sports Illustrated*'s Sportsman of the Year Award for 1978; and *Sports Illustrated*'s Athlete of the Decade Award in 1980.

Nicklaus' family life comes before anything else for him. He and his wife Barbara have five children, and their oldest son is also a professional golfer.

61. MARIO ANDRETTI
b. 1940 (Auto Racer)

Mario Andretti

He is the only driver to have won the Daytona 500 (1967), the Indy 500 (1969) and the Formula One World Championship (1978). **Mario Andretti** was born on February 28, 1940, in Montona, an Italian village on the Adriatic Sea. In 1945, Montona became part of Yugoslavia, so the Andrettis moved to Lucca, where he learned about races and race cars. He went to see the run of the Mille Miglia as a boy, and he and his brother Aldo were hooked. With a motorcycle and a small coupe at their disposal, they went racing.

In 1955, the family moved to Nazareth, Pennsylvania. The brothers worked as mechanics and bought a modified 1948 Hudson to run on the stock car ovals. Brother Aldo was the ace driver, but faded from the effort after a serious accident at the track in Hatfield, Pennsylvania. Mario came on strong, however, running modifieds, midgets and three-quarter midgets, working as a mechanic by day and racing by night. On Labor Day, 1963, he won three of four at Hatfield, and four straight at Flemington, New Jersey, on the same day. He decided he was ready for the big time.

His first United States Auto Club Indy car ride resulted in a spinout; but Dean Van Lines racing team chief mechanic Clint Brawner was impressed by Andretti's driving, and offered him a car for the last few races of 1964. Andretti led in two races, but 1965 would be his true rookie year. Driving a Hawk-Ford Indy Car, he had the fastest time for the first qualifying heats of the Indianapolis 500; and finished third in the Indy 500.

He became the USAC points champion that year, becoming one of very few rookie Champions with one win and 10 finishes in the top four in 17 races. In 1966, he was points champion again, also setting a record by leading 500 consecutive miles of championship racing by winning the At-lanta 300, Milwaukee 100 and the Langhorne 100 — winning eight of 15 that year. He was on his way.

He moved into Championship GT cars, running a Ferrari. He won Sebring, then set a new lap record at Le Mans of 3:23.6; he also went CanAm racing.

He won the 1967 Daytona 500 in a Holman & Moody-prepared Ford Fairlane. In an intense race that saw nine flags for accidents, Andretti took the lead for a caution flag, chanced running out of fuel to save pit stop time, and fought his way from a 12th-place start to victory over such legends as Fred Lorenzen, Paul Goldsmith, Cale Yarbrough and Curtis Turner.

Andretti went on to more wins, some lean times and a lot of racing. Active well into the 1990s, he concentrated on Indy Car racing in his later years. Rounding out his record are four USAC/CART Championships; the 1965 Indy 500 Rookie of the Year award; and second-place on the all-time win list for Indy Cars, with 51 victories. His son Michael is also a champion race car driver, setting records in the footsteps of his father.

62. PELE
b. 1940 (Soccer Player)

Pele was born **Edson Arantes do Nascimento** in Tres Coracoes, Brazil, on October 23, 1940. His father was a soccer pro, but his bad knees forced him to retire, and when Pele was four, they moved to Bauru.

Pele and the neighborhood children played soccer from dawn to dusk, with a sock stuffed with newspapers wadded into a ball shape. His father coached him, and Pele and his friends played other boy's teams from other neighborhoods.

Soon, Pele was playing on the junior squad of the Bauru city team, which he led to the junior championship for each of the next three years. Then he signed with Santos, an important pro team. He scored a league-record 17 goals in his first year. He was chosen for the Brazilian World Cup team in 1958. Brazil won the World Cup,

Pele

beating Sweden 5-2 in the final.

The victory, as were many to come, was in large part due to Pele's extraordinary level of play. The ball seemed connected to his feet as if by a string; he could kick it straight or curve it right or left, he could flick it back and forth at a dead run; he had a thousand moves to break a trap, or get the ball to his teammates; he seemed to know what was going on everywhere on the field; he was a master strategist; he could kick or head the ball with pinpoint accuracy; he could bank the ball off an opponent for a goal; and he held every major scoring record in soccer-mad Brazil.

In the 1970s, a war between Biafra and Nigeria halted for two days because both sides wanted to see Pele play. Pope Paul VI once said to him, "Don't be nervous, my son. I am more nervous than you, for I have been waiting to meet Pele personally for a long time."

After leading Brazil to three World Cup Championships, he retired from the Brazilian national team in 1970. He played for Santos; then announced his second retirement on October 2, 1974. However, Clive Toye, president of the New York City Cosmos, had been begging him to play in the US and "go down in history as the man who truly brought soccer to the United States."

He played for the Cosmos from 1975 to 1978, all the time infusing the US with the excitement of soccer. Cosmos games averaged 40,000 attendance in 1977. Pele *had* brought soccer to the United States.

When he retired from professional play, there were 761 journalists from 25 countries, heads of state and other renowned public figures on hand to say farewell to Pele, soccer's "magical figure," as he was often described. He had scored 1282 goals in 22 years, and been his sport's ambassador to the world.

Margaret Smith Court became only the second woman to win the tennis Grand Slam for singles play — the US Open, the French Open, the Australian Open and Wimbledon — in 1970, the year after the first woman to accomplish that feat, Maureen Connolly, passed away.

Her win at Wimbledon was especially dramatic, capping an extraordinary 46-game final. She defeated Billie Jean King for the title. This was not her *first* Grand Slam win, however. She had won it for mixed doubles play, with Ken Smith, in 1963 as well.

She was the greatest woman tennis player Australia had known to that date. Meanwhile, her husband Barry, their children Danny and Marika *and* their nanny, travelled with her on the circuit.

She won her first international tournament, the US Singles Championship, in 1962. Then she won Wimbledon, and then got married. She had planned on retiring then, but, with the encouragement of her husband, she played on.

By 1973, she had 61 major championship wins, including three Wimbledons and five US Nationals. That same year, she was points winner and high money winner on the Virginia Slims circuit, with winnings of $180,058.

By the time of her retirement, she had won 26 major tournament singles titles: 11 Australian, seven US, five French and three Wimbledon. She is the all-time winner in Grand Slam Singles Championships, with 26 wins; and total Grand Slam event victories, with 66.

Margaret Smith Court

64. MUHAMMAD ALI
b. 1942 (Boxer)

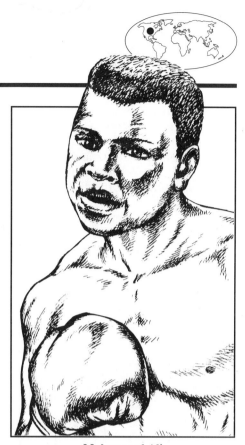
Muhammad Ali

He was the only three-time World Heavyweight Champion, and had a career record of 56 wins and five losses, with 37 knockouts and 19 title defenses. He was born **Cassius Clay** on January 17, 1942, in Louisville, Kentucky. When he was 12 he took up boxing. He'd get up at dawn to run; then he'd jog alongside the school bus to school; then he would run again at lunchtime. Evenings, he skipped rope, worked out on the heavy bag and the speed bag, and shadow boxed at Martin's gym.

From ages 12 to 18, Clay fought in more than 100 amateur fights. He won the Light-Heavyweight divison national Golden Gloves (1959) and the Amateur Athletic Union (1959 and 1960) championships. Also in 1960, he won Olympic Gold.

He signed on with a Louisville boxing syndicate to become a pro. With Angelo Dundee as his trainer, he won his first pro fight, on October 29, 1960, over Tunney Hunsaker. By fall 1962, he had won 16 straight. He was six feet three, and very quick. He also talked fast, making up rhymes to predict the outcome of the fight.

He was popular for his brashness, and for his obvious ability. He KO'd Archie Moore in four rounds; he beat English heavyweight champ Henry Cooper. In February 1964, he beat Sonny Liston for the Heavyweight Championship of the World in seven rounds. He beat Liston in the rematch, with the ultra-quick "punch nobody saw," in one round.

Soon after, he became a Muslim, changing his name to **Muhammad Ali**. He said his religion forbade him to bear arms, and he was branded a draft evader during the Vietnam War. He was stripped of his title and barred from boxing for three and one-half years. When the courts finally exonerated him, he went after the champion in his absence, Joe Frazier, on March 8, 1971. It was billed as the "Fight of the Century." Each

boxer got $2.5 million. Frazier won in 15 rounds. Ali fought 14 times in the following three years, losing once, to Ken Norton, who he then beat in a rematch. He fought Frazier again, and won — but by then Frazier had lost the title to George Foreman.

On March 30, 1974, in Kinasha, Zaire, Ali fought Foreman for the title, in what Ali called "The Rumble in the Jungle." Foreman was seven years younger, and had never been knocked off his feet in a fight, but Ali knocked him out in eight rounds. He next fought Frazier a third time in the "Thrilla in Manila," outslugging Frazier for the win.

On February 15, 1978, he lost the title to Leon Spinks, who was 12 years younger. Ali beat Spinks in the rematch, to win back his title a record third time. He retired in 1979, only to come back for one more fight, a loss against Larry Holmes.

65. VASILI ALEXEYEV
b. 1942 (Weightlifter)

Vasili Alexeyev was the greatest weightlifter in the history of the USSR. He won the Gold Medal at two consecutive Olympic Games, in 1972 and 1976, was also World Champion eight times, and was unbeaten in competition from 1970 to 1978.

Many devoted weightlifters labor in obscurity. Especially those in the super-heavyweight division lack the kind of sleek, well-defined musculature that makes for a romantic media star. Instead, most upper-division weightlifters look much like overweight accountants, except that their bulk tends to be solid masses of muscle, built for strength and not for show.

Just so Vasili Alexeyev. One morning during a competition, he was seen having a breakfast of 26 fried eggs and a steak. Even so, he was lovable, the proof being his marriage in 1962 to a woman named — presciently — Olympiada. Every man should love his work so much!

Alexeyev strolled into the international limelight on June 24, 1970, when he broke the World Record for the press, the jerk and the three-lift combined weight. He also became the first person in recorded history to lift a combined total of 1339.25 pounds. In September 1970, he jerked a weight in excess of 500 pounds, breaking a weightlifting barrier as significant as the four-minute mile in running.

At the 1972 Olympics, in Munich, he was 30 years old and weighed 337 pounds — in the peak of condition. His press, snatch, jerk and combined weight lift were all Olympic records, at 519, 386, 507 and 1411, for the Gold.

In Montreal, at the 1976 Olympics, he set an Olympic record for the snatch at 408 pounds, and a World record for the jerk at 562 pounds, with a total combined weight of 970 pounds (the press was no longer used in the competition).

From 1970-1977, Alexeyev set 80 world records. He was injured in the 1978 World Championship, and was forced into a decline by his injury. Even so, he will be remembered as the man who broke significant barriers for weightlifters everywhere.

Vasili Alexeyev

66. PHIL ESPOSITO
b. 1942 (Hockey Player)

Born on February 20, 1942, in Sault Sainte Marie, Ontario, **Philip Anthony Esposito** became known as simply "Espo." Everyone knew his name, and no wonder: he was the first to break the 100-point barrier with 126 points for the 1969 season; scoring over 100 points in each of six seasons. He led the NHL in goals for six consecutive years; points five and assists, three years.

He was an All-Star six times; he is fourth in All-Time points, with 1590; and goals, with 717. He won the Most Valuable Player Award in 1969 and 1974; scored over 30 goals for 13 consecutive seasons; and was an All-Star six times. With 873 assists, he is fifth All-Time. His 1282 games played was second All-Time. He won the Art Ross Trophy for the Top Scorer in the league in 1969, 1971, 1972, 1973 and 1974.

He played center, and in his first season, 1962-1963, played for a Black Hawk farm team, moving up to the big time in Chica-

Phil Esposito

go in 1963-1964, and becoming a regular the year after. He was traded to the Boston Bruins in 1967. In 1975, the New York Rangers traded for him.

He retired in 1981, and did television commentary for Ranger games. He became the Rangers' general manager from 1986 to 1989, and moved on to become the general manager of the Tampa Bay team.

Lawrence Mahan was born on November 21, 1943 in Brooks, Oregon, and was to become the All-Around Champion five times consecutively (a record), from 1966-1970, as well as a separate win in 1973.

Mahan began riding in the rodeo at a children's competition in 1956; in 1962, he won the All-Around Cowboy Oregon Championship, as well as the bareback bronc riding and bulldogging events.

He joined the Rodeo Cowboys Association in 1963, and began winning often in his specialties of bareback bronc and saddle bronc riding, and bull riding — for the latter, he was top money winner in 1965.

Larry Mahan

In 1966, he was the first cowboy to compete in three Rodeo Nationals final events. This was the beginning of his five-year streak of repeats for the All-Around Cowboy title.

Mahan was one of the first rodeo stars to buy his own airplane for transportation from event to event in the busy rodeo season schedule. He became the first rodeo star to earn more than $50,000 in a year, in 1967. By 1971, his career earnings were in excess of $280,000 — another record. One of the most popular of all rodeo champions, he became a media star as well, appearing in motion pictures, television dramas and promotional vignettes.

He was injured in the early 1970s, which slowed him down a bit. After he won his last All-Around Championship in 1973, he retired to spend more time at his rodeo schools for youngsters and tending to his signature line of Western clothing, taking time for breaks at his Arizona ranch near Phoenix.

Inventor of the "sweeper" position in soccer, he was also a leading proponent of a new style of soccer that came into focus in the early 1970s. This new style was called "total soccer," and it meant that any player had to be ready to function wherever they were on the field.

Franz Beckenbauer was born on September 11, 1945 in what was to become West Germany. He was to prove himself an outstanding innovator and a brilliant team leader. He captained the West German team to the World Cup Championship in 1974, and showed his versatility by coaching the West German team to the World

Franz Beckenbauer

Cup Championship again in 1990.

This represented two of West Germany's three World Cup wins. Soccer, for all of its running and kicking and heading of the ball, is often a war of defense, a war of nerves.

The 1974 championship game was West Germany against Holland — an exciting match, because the two contenders were the leading proponents of the new "total soccer" concept of play. Beckenbauer's counterpart for Holland was Johan Cruyf. Holland's Johann Neeskens scored in the first minute of the game on a penalty kick. Germany's Paul Breitner scored in the 25th minute of the game — also on a penalty kick — and his teammate Gerd Muller scored at 43 minutes to put the game away. The final score was Germany, 2-1.

He won the European Player of the Year Award twice, in 1972 and 1976, while playing for West Germany, tying with KH Rummenigge (who won it in 1980 and 1981) for the honors of leading his nation in that respect.

Beckenbauer went on to play in the United States for the New York Cosmos in 1977, 1978, 1979, 1980 and 1983. This was during an increased interest in soccer in America that was precipitated by the appearance in the ranks of the New York Cosmos of **Pele (see no. 62)**, just shortly before Beckenbauer joined the team.

In 1977, Beckenbauer was voted the North American Soccer League Player of the Year. The Cosmos won the NASL Championship in 1977, 1978 and 1980, finishing second in 1981, when the Chicago Sting scored one goal for the tie breaker.

In 1990, with Beckenbauer as coach, the German natioanl team blanked Argentina 1-0, on one goal scored by Andreas Brehme. It was a penalty kick in the 85th minute of the game.

The greatest Japanese gymnast in history was born on October 11, 1946. He worked hard, practicing his gymnastics as he took part in the competitive spirit that would make Japan a leading Olympic contender from the late 1960s on.

Sawao Kato won eight Olympic Gold Medals in gymnastics — more than any other male gymnast, in the 1968 Olympics in Mexico City, the 1972 Olympics in Munich and in the 1976 Olympics, held in Montreal. He also won three Silver and one Bronze in those competitions, ranking seventh on the list of All-Time Olympic Medal Winners (men and women included) as of 1994.

He won the All-Around in 1968 and 1972; with points totals of 115.9 and 114.65, respectively. He also won the Gold for the Parallel Bars in 1972 and 1976, with points totals of 19.475 and 19.675.

He won the Gold for the Floor Exercise in 1968, with a points total of 19.475. In addition, he was part of the Japanese team that won the Gold for Team Combined Exercises in Gymnastics in 1968 and 1972 (the Japanese team won this event from 1960 through 1976). His other Olympic victories included two Silver Medals in the 1972 Olympics, in the Side Horse exercise and the Horizontal Bars; and one Bronze Medal in the 1968 Olympics.

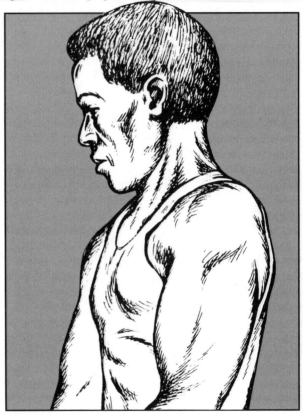

Sawao Kato

This five-time Eclipse Award winner (more than any other person) is second only to **Willie Shoemaker (see no. 50)** in career wins, with a total approaching 8000. To date, he has won three Belmont Stakes Championships and six Breeder's Cups. **Laffit Pincay, Jr.** has also won one Kentucky Derby, aboard the fabulous thoroughbred Swale, in 1984. The Kentucky Derby win was run in 2:02.4, over thoroughbreds Coax Me Chad, who ran second and At the Threshold, finishing third.

The Belmont Stakes wins took place in three consecutive years. The first was aboard Conquistador Cielo, in 1982, for a time of 2:28.2, over second- and third-place finishers Gato del Sol and Illuminate. In 1983, Pincay won while riding Caveat, for a time of 2:27.8, defeating Slew O' Gold and Barberstown, who ran second and third, respectively. The third Belmont Stakes win was aboard Swale in 1984. Swale ran 2:27.2, leaving competitors Pine Circle and Morning Bob in second and third place.

He was nominated the Outstanding Jockey of the Year in 1971, 1973-74, 1979 and 1985 — a record number of times winning that award. Pincay also topped the record for career winnings, with $170, 325, 931 as of 1994.

Laffit Pincay, Jr.

He is also second only to Shoemaker in years leading his colleagues in terms of winnings per year, with totals in the years 1970 to 1974, 1979 and 1985 of $2,626,526; $3,784,377; $3,225,827; $4,093,492; $4,251,060; $8,183,535; and $13,415,049, respectively.

The Breeder's Cup is run to determine thoroughbred racing's principal champions, in a series of seven races run in one day late in the season. The length of the race run has varied in distance from one to 1.5 miles over the years.

Pincay won in 1985 in the Juvenile Thoroughbred category, at Aqueduct, aboard Tasso, in 1:36.2 for the mile, leaving behind Storm Cat and Scat Dancer. He won again at Santa Anita, in 1986, riding Capote, outrunning Qualify and Alysheba for a time of 1:43.8 for 1.06 miles. He won again on Is It True, going the 1.06 miles in 1:46.6 to beat Easy Goer and Tagel, in 1988.

He also won the Breeder's Cup Distaff race aboard Bayakoa in 1989 and 1990, going the 1.125 miles in 1:472.5 and 1:491.5, respectively. Riding Skywalker, Pincay won the Breeder's Cup Classic in 2:00.4 in 1986, at Santa Anita. As of the 1992 season, Pincay was second in All-Time Breeder's Cup money winners, with 51 starts for $6.235 million.

71. KAREEM ABDUL-JABBAR
b. 1947 (Basketball Player)

He was born **Lew Ferninand Alcindor** on April 16, 1947 in New York City. His name would change. What didn't change was his quiet, subdued demeanor, which he would carry through his career.

He first played basketball in fourth grade, at St. Jude's parochial grade school, which took part in the Catholic Youth Organization's grammar school basketball program. He worked hard at learning the findamentals of the game, putting in long hours because he wanted to excel at the game. By the time he attended high school at Power Memorial High, he was six feet ten inches tall — and still growing.

Coach Jack Donohue had a winning program going in New York's Catholic basketball league: Alcindor fit in perfectly. In his second year there, he averaged just over 19 points per game, for a total of 515 points plus 444 rebounds with a 53 percent shooting average from the field. Power Memorial won 27 games, plus the Catholic high school league championship. In his senior year, Power had 71 victories in a row on its way to winning the Catholic league championship again. Alcindor set a New York City record for high school career points at 2067 and rebounds at 2002, and was also among the leading students academically.

Coach Donohue monitored press, recruiter and scout access to the young star throughout his high school career. Despite mounting pressure to join the pros, Alcindor went to college instead.

In his first game for UCLA, he led the freshman team in a 75-60 win over the two-time national champion varsity team, scoring 31 points himself. He became a Muslim just after his junior year, changing his name to **Kareem Abdul-Jabbar**.

He led UCLA to three national titles, in 1967, 1968 and 1969, and was named Most Valuable Player of the NCAA play-

Kareem Abdul-Jabbar

offs three times, and College Player of the Year twice.

He began his pro career with the Milwaukee Bucks, leading leading them to the National Basketball Association championship in 1971. He then played for the Los Angeles Lakers, leading them to five NBA championships. He was nominated Most Valuable Player eight times: twice for the playoffs in 1971 and 1985, and six times for the regular season, in 1971, 1972, 1974, 1976, 1977 and 1980.

He retired after 20 seasons, having set the record for All-Time leader in points scored, with 38,387; field goal attempts/completions, 28,307/15,837; blocked shots, 3189; games played, 1560, and years played; in fact, he retired as All-Time leader in 20 categories.

72. DAN GABLE
b. 1948 (Wrestler)

Born on October 25, 1948, **Daniel Gable** was a two-time National Collegiate Athletics Association champion, in 1968-1969. He was voted the tourney's Most Outstanding Wrestler in 1969. His collegiate wrestling record for the 137-pound class was 118 wins to one loss, while wrestling for coach Harold Nichols at Iowa State.

Gable went to the 1972 Olympics in Munich, and won the Gold Medal for the Lightweight Class (149 pounds) in Freestyle Wrestling, besting Silver Medalist Kikuo Wada, of Japan; and Bronze Medalist Rusi Ashuraliev, of the USSR.

He then began a career at the University of Iowa as a wrestling coach, producing teams that won nine straight NCAA Intercollegiate Wrestling Championships in 1978, 1979, 1980, 1981, 1982, 1983, 1984, 1985 and 1986. He added three more championships in 1991, 1992 and 1993.

He also returned to the Olympics, as the coach of the US Freestyle Wrestling Team in 1988, in Seoul. The team's Featherweight and Welterweight contenders, John Smith and Ken Monday, won Gold Medals; Superheavyweight Bruce Bumgartner won Silver; and Lightweight and Heavyweight wrestlers Nate Carr and William Scherr won Bronze in their divisons. Gable's rugged training style, which sometimes included five daily sessions, enabled him to enjoy an excellent career in which he lost only one bout.

Dan Gable

73. MARK SPITZ
b. 1950 (Swimmer)

Mark Spitz

The first athlete to win seven Gold Medals in a single Olympic Games, **Mark Spitz** was born on February 10, 1950 in Modesto, California.

He won two Gold medals in team relay races in the Mexico City Olympics of 1968, plus a Silver and a Bronze. The Golds were in the 400-meter and 800-meter Freestyle Relays. At that competition, however, he caused controversy by predicting he'd win six medals. He would have to wait four more years for his prognostication to become true.

His training took place at the Santa Clara Swim Club in California, where many ambitious US swimmers have trained.

He won the Sullivan Award as the Number One Amateur Athlete in the US, in 1971. In 1972, he graduated from Indiana University. He captained the university's swim team — which had won, and would go on to win, the NCAA Division I Team Championship in 1968, 1969, 1970, 1971, 1972 and 1973.

Spitz made history in the 1972 Olympics in Munich. He set world records and won the Gold Medal for all four individual events he entered. In the 100-meter Freestyle, he set a record of 51.2 seconds. He set another record of 1:52.8 in the 200-meter Freestyle. He won the 100-meter Butterfly competition in a record 54.3 seconds, and set a fourth record in winning the 200-meter Butterfly in 2:07.

He won three more Golds as a member of US team victories in the 400-meter Freestyle Relay; the 800-meter Freestyle Relay; and the 400-meter Medley Relay. These wins were also in record times.

He was much in demand as a media personality after this historic feat. He attempted a comeback in 1991, but time had taken its toll, and he did not compete in the 1992 Olympics as he had hoped to do.

Mark Spitz set 23 World and 35 US swimming records, and is the All-Time Gold Medal winner in a single Olympics. He was entered into the Olympics Hall of Fame in 1983.

74. GUSTAVO THOENI
b. 1951 (Skier)

One of the greatest Alpine skiers, **Gustavo Thoeni**, was born in Italy on February 28, 1951. He was the first four-time World Cup Overall Champion, in 1971, 1972, 1973 and 1975, breaking that ground for successors **Primin Zurbriggen (see no. 98)** and Marc Ghirardelli. He is, to date, the only Italian World Cup Overall Champion.

His specialties were the Slalom and the Giant Slalom, both events demanding speed, agility and a fierce competitive spirit.

While the downhill race is a contest of sheer speed and cornering, over a vertical course of 2625 feet (for Men's World Cup competition), the Slalom emphasizes technical virtuosity.

The winner of the Downhill is determined by a single run. The winner of the Slalom is determined by totalling two separate runs. The race is run over a switchback-style course, demanding quick, short turns through various combinations of gates.

In Men's competition, there are 55 to 75 gates, and the length of the course is comparatively short, at 459 to 722 feet for men; and 40-60 gates for Women's competition, on a course ranging from 394 to 722 feet.

In Giant Slalom, the gates are farther apart and fewer, and the race is run on a longer course, from 820 to 1312 feet for men, and 820 to 984 feet for women. Again, the total of both runs determines the winner.

Thoeni was one of the "new breed" of Italian Alpine skiers, specializing in Slalom events, and producing Thoeni and another "genius of the gates," Alberto Tomba.

In addition to the above accomplishments, Thoeni also won a Gold Medal in the Giant Slalom at the 1972 Sapporo Olympics; silvering in the Slalom that same year; and in 1976, at Innsbruck, he won the Silver Medal in the Slalom.

These were accompanied by his winning two FIS World Alpine Ski Championships, at the legendary ski slopes of St. Moritz, in 1974: he won the FIS Championship for the Slalom and the FIS Championship for the Giant Slalom there.

In World Cup competition, in addition to the Overall Championships, Thoeni won the Championship in the Slalom in 1973 and 1974; and the Championship in the Giant Slalom in 1970 and 1972.

Gustavo Thoeni

75. NIKOLAI ANDRIANOV
b. 1952 (Gymnast)

Born on October 14, 1952, **Nikolai Andrianov** grew up under the tutelage of the intensive Soviet academy system, in which children who showed an aptitude for a sport or career were immersed in that activity on up through adulthood.

Andrianov became one of the few men to win seven Gold Medals in Oympic Gymnastics. He won his first Olympic Gold Medal in 1972, when the Games were held in Munich, in the Floor Exercise, with 19.175 points. He won over very strong Japanese competition — Akinori Nakayama, who Silvered (but won the Gold in the Rings), and Shigeru Kasamatsu, who won the Bronze (and the Silver in the Parallel Bars and the Bronze in the Horizontal Bars). He himself also took the Bronze Medal in the Long Horse competition.

He has the All-Time record for most Men's medals taken in Olympic Competition, with 15.

The 1972 Olympics took place in the 16th year of a 20-year Japanese dominance of Men's Olympic Gymnastics, a period that included the tremendous accomplishments of the great **Sawao Kato (see no. 69)**. The Russians, on the other hand, were laying the groundwork for their own period of Men's Gymnastics dominance — which would begin full-force in 1976, with Andrianov leading the charge for a growing number of USSR and Eastern-bloc victories — and would stretch over the decades well into the 1990s. (In Women's Gymnastics, the USSR and the Eastern bloc had been dominant since 1948.)

Andrianov took on his role as a groundbreaker for this gathering Gymnastics power in a winning fashion. In the next Olympics, Andrianov advanced the USSR's aspirations by winning Gold in the All-Around Championship in 1976, in Montreal, with 116.65 points overall, best-

Nikolai Andrianov

ing Sawao Kato, who came in with the Silver.

That same Olympics, he won the Gold in the Vault competition, with 19.45 points. He also won Gold in the Rings competition, with 19.65 points, to defeat his countryman, the rising star on the Soviet horizon, Alexander Dityatin. He rounded out his Golds for that year by winning in the Floor Exercise, with 19.45 points.

He came in second to Kato in the Parallel Bars, and third in the Side Horse. The Japanese won the Team Combined Gold for the fifth straight Olympics, but the Russians were clearly on the march.

In 1980, at Moscow, the USSR won the Team Combined; Alexander Dityatin won the All-Around and the Rings; Alexander Tchachiev took the Gold in the Parallel Bars; Andrianov took the Gold in the Vault competition; and the Eastern bloc won eight Golds in eight events. Andrianov had done his job well.

Born September 2, 1952, **James Scott Conners** took an early interest in tennis. The apocryphal tale of his childhood says that, by his third birthday, his mother put a tennis racquet in his hands, and had him practicing. At seven, he was taking lessons.

By the time he turned pro, he was being coached by Pancho Segura. He was the National Collegiate Athletics Association champion in 1971, and he was rated Number One in the World in 1974, 1975, 1976, 1977 and 1978.

He would, in his career, set All-Time records in professional singles championships won, with 109; Wimbledon matches won, at 84; and US Open matches won, at 98. He took the Championship at Wimbledon twice; won the Australian Open Championship once; and won five US Open Championships between 1974 and 1983.

Apart from his high level of play, Connors set himself apart by his abrasive personality: criticizing linemen, cursing at hecklers, arguing with officials and pointedly angering his peers in the tennis world by mocking some, suing others for perceived insults, delaying service or rushing it with others, and a battery of quirks and sour nuances that belied the tennis tradition of its being a genteel game.

He was the more publicized of a duo of behavioral miscreants that also included the sharp-tempered Romanian Ilye Nastase. Sportswriter Glenn Dickey, in his book *Champs and Chumps*, blames some or most of this behavior to the influence of Connors' manager (who believed in shock tactics) his youth. He was talking wearily of retirement as early as age 22, when his earnings from tennis were already in or near seven digits. By the 1980s, he had mellowed with age and marriage.

Essentially, Connors plays a highly ag-gressive game of tennis: every stroke is hard, an insistent pressure that finds the weakness in his opponent's game. His return of service is unparalelled. A strong serve his way will come back to the opponent just as hard as it was originally hit.

He is also one of few sports stars to convincingly attempt a comeback. He was in the Top 10 rankings up to and including 1988. He backed away from tennis in 1989. When he made moves to come out of retirement, he was seeded 936th in the world in December 1990. In 1991, he had made it to the semifinals at the US Open.

Jimmy Connors

83

Born **Annemarie Moser** on March 27, 1953, in Kleinarl, Austria, she began skiing at four years of age, a natural turn of events for an Austrian child of the time. When she was 15, she was ready for the Austrian National Ski Team.

Moser-Proell won the World Cup All-Around Ski Championship six times, more than any other skier — an epithet that would be applied to several of her accomplishments.

An extraordinary skier, she won the Women's World Cup Downhill Championship an All-Time record seven times, from and including 1971-1975, and 1978-1979. She won the World Cup Giant Slalom three times, in 1971, 1972 and

1975. She won the World Cup Combined in 1979 (a tie for first with Hanni Wenzel, of Liechtenstein).

Her name became hyphenated, changing from Annemarie Moser to Annemarie Moser-Proell, between the seasons of 1973 and 1974, when she was married. This life-changing event did not slow her down competitively, however. It happened in the midst of her famous record five consecutive wins of the World Cup Overall Championship. Altogether, she won it six times for another record: in 1971, 1972, 1973, 1974, 1975 and 1979.

She also scored an All-Time record 33 lifetime wins in World Cup Downhill events; a second-best All-Time record of 16 wins in the World Cup Giant Slalom; and another second-best All-Time record of seven wins in World Cup Combined events.

She retired in 1976. In 1978, she returned to competition, the results of which can be seen above. This comeback also included a Gold Medal in the Downhill Ski Championship at the 1980 Olympic Games at Lake Placid. She re-entered retirement after the Olympics.

Annemarie Moser-Proell

78. RAISA SMETANINA
b. 1953 (Skier)

Raisa Smetanina is the top All-Time Winter Olympics medal winner with 10 Cross-Country Skiing medals — four Gold, five Silver and a Bronze, won over the span of five Winter Olympic games in 1976, 1980, 1984, 1988 and 1992 in her appearances for the USSR and the Unified Team.

In the 1976 Olympics at Innsbruck, Smetanina won the Gold Medal in the Women's 10-Kilometer Cross-Country Skiing event; and won the Silver Medal in the Five-Kilometer Cross-Country. Both were tight contests with Helen Tukkalo of Finland. She won another Gold as part of the USSR Women's 20-Kilometer Relay team.

In 1980, at the Olympics at Lake Placid, she won the Gold Medal in the Women's Five-Kilometer Cross-Country race, bettering Hikka Riihivuori, of Finland, who won the Silver. She also picked up a Silver Medal as a member of the USSR Women's 20-Kilometer Relay team.

Smetanina won two Silver Medals in the 1984 Olympics in Sarajevo, coming in second in the Women's 10-Kilometer Cross-Country race; as well as in the Women's 20-Kilometer Cross-Country race. In both instances, she was bettered by Gold Medalist Marja-Liisa Hamalainen, of Finland.

Smetanina won a Gold Medal as part of the USSR Women's 20-Kilometer Relay team; and she won her record ninth medal, a Bronze, in the Women's 20-Kilometer Cross-Country race, at the 1988 Olympics in Calgary.

Raisa Smetanina

79. CHRIS EVERT
b. 1954 (Tennis Player)

Born December 21, 1954, in Fort Lauderdale, Florida, **Christine Marie Evert** grew up in a family where tennis was a passion. Her father and her four siblings were all dedicated players: the kids won competitions, and Dad coached them. Chris had her first racquet when she was five, and developed a dedicated practice routine. She entered every age-group competition available. By the time she was 12, she was ranked Number Two nationally for that age group; at 14 and 16, she was ranked Number One nationally for those age groups.

The season of her 16th birthday, she won 46 straight singles victories. Then she debuted at the US Open at Forest Hills, making it to the semifinals, establishing a record as the youngest woman to do so. At 17, she won the $100,000 Virginia Slims Tournament at Boca Raton — the richest women's tournament of the time.

She was seemingly aloof — but it was a mental shield developed to protect her still-young self against the intensities of such elevated competition. As she grew older, she became warmer personally, despite a frustrating on-again, off-again romance with fellow tennis star **Jimmy Connors (see no. 76)**.

1973 was her first year as a pro. She won six of seven tournaments she entered. Her second pro year, she won 15 tournaments, including Wimbledon, the Canadian Open and the French Open.

In 1974, she was the Associated Press Woman Athlete of the Year. She was ranked Number One in 1975, and won her first US Open title, over the great Australian champion, Evonne Goolagong — 5-7, 6-4, 6-2. She had 76 clay-court victories in a row that year.

She went on to establish one of the greatest tennis careers of all time — which is especially remarkable in light of the fact

Chris Evert

that she retired while still ranked among tennis' Top Ten Women Players, to raise a family — an idea that had been developing ever since she had gotten married to become Chris Evert-Lloyd.

She established a record in tournament victories at 157 wins; she won at least one Grand Slam singles championship each year from 1974 to 1986. She is the third all-time in Womens' Grand Slam singles championships (as of 1994, tied with **Martina Navratilova [see no. 84]**). She won two Australian Opens; three Wimbledons; six US Opens; and seven French Opens.

She was a superb tennis champion, and like many great champions, she also had a great rival, Martina Navratilova. As it was, she established a new level of competition in Women's Tennis, garnering increased respect for, and interest in, the sport.

80. CHIP HANAUER
b. 1954 (Power Boat Racer)

Born on July 1, 1954, **Chip Hanauer** is the most dominant driver in contemporary American power boat racing. He is the first unlimited hydroplane pilot to win the sport's top trophy, the American Power Boat Association Gold Cup for Unlimited Hydroplane, nine times. He also owns the longest streak of consecutive Gold Cup Championships, continuous from 1982 through 1988.

Unlimited hydroplane racing is one of the most spectacular motorsports, involving boats that incorporate the latest racing hull design and technology, coupled with the latest advances in getting the absolute maximum power out of a large, automotive-type engine, and transferring that power to the water.

While the sport is rather obscure to the average fan of baseball, basketball and football, it is a fact that the American Power Boat Association Gold Cup for Unlimited Hydroplane is the oldest motor sports trophy still in active competition in the US.

From 1917 to 1921, a driver named Gar Wood seemed invincible as he piloted his race-prepared motor boats *Miss Detroit* (II and III) and *Miss America* to a string of five consecutive APBA Gold Cups. The century was still young; the media was more open-handed with its coverage; and Gar Wood was a household name in the United States. The speeds he attained ranged from 42 to 61 mph.

Bill Muncey, driving *Miss Thriftaway*, then *Miss Century 21*, and then the *Atlas Van Lines Special*, established a dynasty of his own — eight APBA Gold Cups, strung out over 23 years, with winning speeds ranging from 97 mph to 112 mph. He dueled in and out of the championship with such powerboat legends as Ron Mussen, driving the legendary *Miss Bardahl* hydroplane; and Dean Chenowith, driving the

Chip Hanauer

famous *Miss Budweiser* hydroplane.

Chip Hanauer began his dominance of the Gold Cup in 1982, driving the *Atlas Van Lines Special* to victory at 120 mph. He drove for wins aboard the *Atlas Van Lines Special* in 1983 and 1984 as well. He switched to Miller American for 1985 through 1987; went with *Miss Circus Circus* in 1988; then went to *Miss Budweiser* again, for a Gold Cup win in 1992.

Then, on 6 June 1993, Hanauer piloted *Miss Budwesier* for a second win, and his record ninth Gold Cup, over a 2.5-mile course on the Detroit River, for a speed of 141.296 mph. In qualifying runs for the same meet, Mark Tate, winner of the 1991 Gold Cup, broke the 170 mph barrier driving the *Winston Eagle*. That boat failed to finish in the final, however.

81. BERNARD HINAULT
b. 1954 (Cyclist)

Born November 15, 1954, **Bernard Hinault** is one of bicycling's great champions. He came to dominate the world's greatest bicycle race, the **Tour de France**, winning it five times, from 1978 to 1985. Hinault was voted the Top French Athlete of the Last 60 Years in 1986.

Hinault won his first Tour de France in 1978, with a time of 108 hours and 18 minutes. In 1979, Hinault won again, in 103:06.50. The race began on June 27, and Hinault crossed the finish line on July 22. The course ran the distance from Leiden, Holland, to Paris, totalling 2200 miles, and the cyclists covered the distance in stages of approximately 100 miles each. In 1980, Hinault dropped out of the Tour with tendinitis. That same year, he was named the Professional Road Race World Champion.

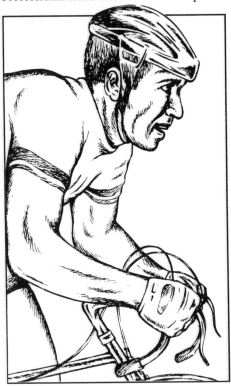

Bernard Hinault

While others (Belgium's Eddy Merckx and Hinault's countryman, Jacques Anquetil) may also have won the Tour de France five times, his times were *consistently* lower than theirs — an indication not only of his own prowess, but also of new organizational thinking in terms of course variations, and obvious improvements in equipment. Those factors, combined with a resurgent interest in the sport of cycling, meant that Bernard Hinault was helping to introduce a new era in long-distance cycling.

The 1981 Tour led from Nice to Paris, a distance of 2325 miles, run in stages of 110 miles each: Hinault won five of these stages, and in doing so, won the race. This year's Tour was contested at a record average speed of 24 miles per hour. Another record for the race was the number of cyclists who finished: 121 out of 150 starters. Hinault's time was 96:19.38.

On July 25, 1982, Hinault won the Tour again. The race took place on the roads leading from Bale, Switzerland, to Paris — a distance of 2181 miles in stages of approximately 100 miles each. In taking the victory, Hinault staged a dramatic come-from-behind charge in the last stage of the race to beat Joop Zoetemelk, of The Netherlands, by 6:21 in that stage, with an overall time of 92:06:46.

Greg LeMond (see no. 92) became the first American to win the Tour when he triumphed over Hinault in the Tour on July 27, 1986. LeMond was riding on the French team with Hinault at the time. Hinault would go on to win the 16-day, 1065-mile Coors Classic, which wound from San Francisco to Boulder, Colorado. LeMond, his teammate on the Red Zinger team, placed second with a time 1:26 slower than Hinault's.

Hinault retired from racing at the age of 32, on November 14, 1986.

Alain Prost, the leading Formula One racing driver in his career, was born in France on February 24, 1955. Prost set a record of 51 Formula One victories, and won Four Formula One driving Championships. Formula One is the highest level of Grand Prix racing, with cars capable of 200 mph running road races.

Ironically, Prost's arch-rival, Ayrton Senna, of Brazil, died in a Formula One crash at the San Marino Grand Prix, in May 1994, just six months after Prost retired in September, 1993. Senna had filled the retired Prost's vacant spot on the Williams-Renault racing team, and was second to Prost in All-Time Grand Prix standings at the time of the crash.

Prost clinched his fourth Formula One driving title — second only to Juan-Manuel Fangio in All-Time wins of that award — when he won the Portugese Grand Prix on Sept 26, 1993, capping an outstanding career with yet another success. He won the World Championship award in 1985 and 1986, driving for the MacLaren TAG Porsche Turbo team; in 1989, with the McLaren Honda team; and in 1993 with Williams-Renault.

Prost is the All-Time Grand Prix winner, with nearly 200 starts, and approximately 20 pole positions, 51 wins, 32 second places and 18 thirds.

Alain Prost

JOE MONTANA
b. 1956 (Football Player)

Joe Montana

Joe Montana is the greatest quarterback to ever play football. In his collegiate career, he led the University of Notre Dame to the National Championship in 1977. Going into the 1993 pro season, he had the All-Time Highest pass rating, at 93.5 efficiency; he was third in career completions, with 2929; fifth in career yards passed, 35,124; and sixth in career passes for touchdowns, with 244. In addition, his passes had an average gain of 7.64 yards; with interceptions a mere .027 of the total.

He led the National Football League in 1981, 1984, 1985, 1987 and 1990, with respective totals of 3565, 3630, 3653, 3054 and 3944 yards, for 19, 28, 17, 31 and 26 touchdowns. He was Super Bowl Most Valuable Player three times — 1982, 1985 and 1990. He has won four Super Bowls, all of them with the San Francisco 49ers, tying the record.

With Montana at the helm, the 49er teams of the 1980s (also featuring wide receiver Jerry Rice and running back Roger Craig) played so well that they completely dominated professional football.

The 49ers under Montana first won Super Bowl XVI, in January 1982, over Boomer Esiason and the Cincinnati Bengals, by a score of 26-21. Going into the game, the 49ers had a 15-3 win record. Montana hit for 14 completions of 22 passes for 157 yards and one touchdown; plus six carries for 18 yards and one touchdown.

In Super Bowl XIX, in which Montana completed 24 of 35 passes for 331 yards and two touchdowns; plus five carries for 59 yards and one touchdown, the 17-1 49ers defeated the Miami Dolphins 38-16. In Super Bowl XXIII in 1989, San Francisco (14-5) beat Cincinnati (17-1) again, 20-16.

Super Bowl XXIV in 1990 saw the 49ers at their most dominant, with Montana at the very peak of his game. They crushed an outstanding Denver Broncos team 55-10. Montana threw 22 completions of 29 passes, for 297 yards and five touchdowns.

The following year, every team in the regular season played against the 49ers with desperate ferocity, lest they would win the Super Bowl again, becoming greatest team in Super Bowl history.

Injuries abounded, not least of which was Montana, who suffered a vicious, helmet-first tackle in the grueling NFC playoff final against the New York Giants, and was taken out of the game. The exhausted Giants won 15-13.

An injury-haunted Montana was traded to Kansas City in 1993. Kansas City dearly needed his talents, and his performance there led the team to an 11-5 record, the AFC West Championship, and a berth in the playoffs. He was ranked number two in NFL passing for the year, with an average of 87.4 for the season.

84. MARTINA NAVRATILOVA
b. 1956 (Tennis Player)

Martina Navratilova was born on October 18, 1956 in Prague, Czechoslovakia. Her parents had an unhappy marriage, divorcing when she was three, and her father died tragically six years later. Her mother loved to play tennis, often taking Martina to the courts with her. She married again, in 1961, to Mike Navratil, and Martina's name changed to Martina Navratilova (adding the Czech suffix for "daughter of"). He spent considerable time with his stepdaughter, bringing an air of happiness to her life.

He first taught her to play tennis, and took her to see **Rod Laver (see no. 59)** play in a tournament. Laver fired her imagination and she determined to be a tennis champion like Laver.

At eight, she competed in her first tournament, making the semifinals. At nine, she began practice under George Parma, Czechoslovakia's great tennis coach.

At 14, she had won the National Championship for her age group; at 17, she was Czechoslovakia's Number One woman player, with three National Women's Championships and the National Junior Championship to her credit. Her winning streak of 74 matches in 1984 is an all-time record.

She went on to one of tennis' greatest careers before she would announce retirement in 1994. She would win 167 singles matches, would win at least 18 Grand Slam singles championships, four US Opens, in 1983, 1984, 1986 and 1987; three Australian Opens, in 1981, 1983 and 1985; and two French Opens, 1982 and 1984.

With 54 Grand Slam event wins, she is second all-time to **Margaret Smith Court**'s **(see no. 63)** 66. She won the doubles Grand Slam, taking Australian, US, Wimbledon and French Opens, with Pam Shriver, in 1984. In fact Navratilova and Shriver combined for a deadly doubles team that would win 109 consecutive matches from 1983 to 1985. She also had a string of Doubles victories playing in tandem with **Chris Evert (see no. 79)**, who was also her chief rival before Evert retired in the mid-1980s.

Navratilova created an aura of invincibility for herself in the Wimbledon with her record nine Singles Championships won there, six of them consecutively — 1982, 1983, 1984, 1985, 1986 and 1987; the others were won in 1978, 1979 and 1990.

In 1975, she became a resident of the United States, and was granted US citizenship in 1981.

Martina Navratilova

91

85. SUGAR RAY LEONARD
b. 1956 (Boxer)

Ray Leonard was born on May 17, 1956, in Wilmington, North Carolina, the fifth of seven children. He became the professional boxing Champion in five different weight classifications: welterweight, junior middleweight, middleweight, light heavyweight and super middleweight.

As an amateur, he was 145-5, with 75 knockouts. He won the National Golden Gloves, two international championships, plus Gold Medals in the Light Welterweight class at the Pan American Games and in the 1976 Olympics at Montreal.

He saw himself as a boxer of precision and strategy.

As a pro, he first took the World Boxing Council welterweight crown, when with a 25-0 pro record, he defeated Wilfred Benitez in 1979; he lost the title to "Fists of Stone" Roberto Duran in June, 1980, winning it back from Duran just five months later, when the bullyish Duran threw up his hands in the fifth round and said "No mas, no mas (no more, no more)!"

He then defeated "Hit Man" Tommy Hearns for the World Boxing Association half of the welterweight championship, with a technical knockout in 1981. His record was now 31-1, with 22 KOs.

When he became pro, Leonard was wary of the usual, exploitative relationship boxers have with managers. An attorney friend set him up with a syndicate which simply loaned him a stake to get rolling, and then signed him to a lucrative, non-exclusive deal with the ABC television network, which would leave him free to do specials for NBC, CBS and cable networks as well.

Before his first championship, he had made an estimated $3 million. The rules of the boxing game had changed, business-wise, and Leonard was the boxer who changed them. He insisted on $1 million for the fight against Benitez, due to his television saleability — and Benitez, be-

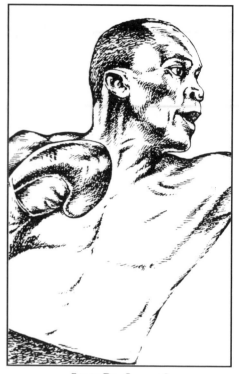

Sugar Ray Leonard

cause he was the champ, had to get even more, by the dictates of tradition: thus, they became the first-ever welterweights to earn $1 million for a single bout.

He was Welterweight Champion in 1979-1980 and 1980-1982; Junior Middleweight Champion in 1981-1982; Middleweight Champion in 1987; WBC Light Heavyweight Champion in 1988; and WBC Super Middleweight Champion in 1988-1990.

His career record was 36-2-1, with 25 knockous. He boxed as a pro from 1977 to 1991 when troubles with a detached retina hastened his retirement. He now gives lectures to youth organizations and citizens groups on brotherhood, good citizenship, the importance of staying in school, good sportsmanship and other positive topics.

86. ERIC HEIDEN
b. 1958 (Speed Skater)

Born on June 14, 1958, in Madison, Wisconsin, **Eric Heiden** started skating at the age of two. As he grew older, his training regimen included running, cycling and weightlifting.

He was the Overall World Champion three times, in 1977, 1978 and 1979. However, he will be most remembered for his unparalleled feat in winning five individual men's Gold Medals, one in each event he entered, at the 1980 Olympics, for which he also was awarded the Sullivan Award as the Top American Amateur Athlete of 1980.

No one has equalled that feat of winning five individual Golds at one Olympics — others, such as **Mark Spitz (see no. 73)**, have won individual *and* team medals for more overall Golds, but Heiden's feat may go unchallenged for some time.

Nor had anyone swept all five men's speed skating events before or since. Heiden's was an epochal accomplishment, setting a lofty standard for any future contender to meet.

In accomplishing this feat, Heiden also set four Olympic records and one world record. He won the 500 meter race in 38.03 seconds, an Olympic record; the 1000 meter race, in 1:15.18, also an Olympic record; the 1500 meter race in 1:55.44, another Olympic record; the 5000 meter race in 7:02.29, also an Olympic record; and the 10,000 meter race in 14.28.13, a World record.

Heiden retired from competitive skating to take up competitive cycling.

Eric Heiden

87. MAGIC JOHNSON
b. 1959 (Basketball Player)

Born on August 14, 1959, **Earvin Johnson** acquired the "Magic" monicker by dint of his deftness with a basketball. He was Most Valuable Player at the NCAA Championships in 1979, as he led Michigan State to a 75-64 victory for the title.

Playing professional basketball for the Los Angeles Lakers, Johnson led the team to five National Basketball Association Championships. He was three-time Most Valuable Player in 1987, 1989 and 1990; and three-time MVP in the playoffs, in 1980, 1982 and 1987.

Leading the league in Assists for an All-Time record of 9921, Johnson was named to the All-NBA first team nine times, eight of those times consecutively.

One of the sport's most engaging personalities, he was a highly popular player, so it came as a shock to basketball fans in 1991 when he announced his retirement, in the prime of his playing life. He cited a positive test for the HIV virus as the reason, because many players felt that playing with or against him in a contact sport was unsafe and doctors advised that he could not physically stand the rigors of an entire NBA season.

Nevertheless, he returned to play the next year, scoring 25 points in the 1992 NBA All-Star game, and rounding out his All-Time playoff records of 2320 assists and 358 steals. Johnson also

played on the USA "Dream Team" that represented the United States at the 1992 Olympics in Barcelona. The Dream Team also featured such stars as Charles Barkley, Larry Bird, Clyde Drexler, Patrick Ewing, **Michael Jordan (see no. 96)**, Karl Malone and other top American players. They won all of their games, including the final, in which they defeated Croatia 117-85.

Before the start of the 1992-93 season, Johnson retired again, to pursue other interests, including a stint as coach of the LA Lakers.

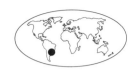

Born on October 30, 1960, **Diego Maradona** set out to do for himself and his country, Argentina, what **Pele (see no. 62)** had done for his native Brazil. He established a reputation for himself as the greatest soccer player in the world in the decade of the 1980s.

In vieing for the World Cup, each country assembles a national team composed of its best native-born players. The qualifying games start two years before the Cup finals, and narrow the field down to 22 teams. The present championship team and the team of the host nation are added to this total, to make a World Cup field of contestants equalling 24 teams. Starting with six groups of four teams, the ensuing playoffs whittle the competition down to two finalists, who compete for the Cup.

Consensus Player of the Decade, he led Argentina to a 1986 World Cup Championship and in 1990, brought them to the finals for the World Cup. Maradona dominated the 1986 World Cup play. His goal-scoring and play-making genius led Argentina to a 3-2 win over West Germany. He was given the Most Valuable Player Award for the 1986 World Cup championship with the Argentina national team.

Maradona also played professional soccer for Naples, Italy, leading their team to win the European Champion Clubs Cup in 1989, the Italian Cup in 1987, and the Championship of the Italian League in 1987 and 1990.

Unfortunately, besides being a great soccer champion, Mardona also exhibited signs of being self-destructive. In March 1991, tested positive for cocaine and was suspended from the game for 15 months by FIFA and the Italian Soccer Federation.

This blot on his brilliant career was worsened by his subsequent loss of a place on the Naples team. He tried a comeback with the Spanish club, Sevilla, but failed when he was habitually absent from practice.

In 1994, he was once again a member of the Argentine national team in World Cup competition. Argentina was given a good chance to win the cup, but when Maradona again failed a drug test and was forced to quit the team, Argentina did not reach the finals.

Diego Maradona

He was the first diver in 56 years to win both the platform and the springboard event in one Olympics, *and* he is the only diver to repeat his Gold Medals wins in those events a second consecutive time. He was also the only diver to score straight perfect 10s in an international competition.

At one point in his career, he held three World Championships, three Pan American Championships, and 48 National titles — which in itself was a record number of Nationals.

Greg Louganis was born on January 29, 1960, adopted shortly after his birth, and raised in El Cajon, California. Both he and his sister, Despina, began dance lessons soon after they could walk. In grade school, Greg added gymnastics to his activities, and then began doing gymnastic-style flips off the family diving board.

His stepfather enrolled him in diving class, and in 1971, he scored a perfect 10 in the AAU Junior Olympics. In 1975, Louganis came under the tutelage of former Olympic diving Gold Medalist Dr Sammy Lee. Louganis went to the 1976 Olympics, in Montreal, at the tender age of 16, winning a Silver Medal in the platform dive.

By Spring of 1978, he had won the one-meter springboard and the 10-meter platform events at the AAU Indoor Diving Championships; the platform championships at the International Hall of Fame Diving Meet; and the Platform Gold Medal at the World Aquatic Championships.

As a student at the University of Miami, he won his first national three-meter springboard championship, beginning a five-year successive dominance of both the one-and -three meter springboard events at the Indoor and Outdoor Diving Championships.

The US boycotted the 1980 Olympics,

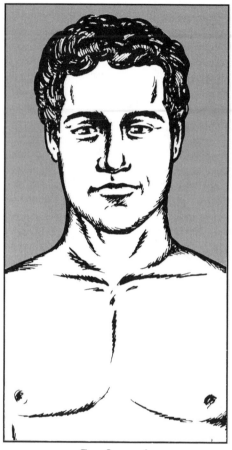

Greg Louganis

where Greg was favored to win the Gold, and he took a break from competitive diving. He switched colleges, to get his Bachelor's Degree in Drama from University of California, Irvine Campus, and to study under the great diving coach Ron O'Brien.

Louganis went on to win the Gold Medals in both springboard and platform diving in the 1984 Olympics, a feat which he repeated in 1988. This would give him a record of four gold medals in Olympic diving competition.

Carl Lewis

When **Carl Lewis** won four Gold Medals at the 1984 Olympic Games, it established his reputation as one of the greatest sprinters of the modern era. He is one of the the world's best and most competitive long-jump athletes, with more than 62 long jumps over 28 feet.

His 9.86-second record for 100 meters was set at the World Championships in Tokyo on August 25, 1991. To date, he has eight Gold Medals in the World Track and Field Championships: three for the 100 meters run, in 1983, 1987 and 1991; three for the 400-meter Relay race, in 1983, 1987 and 1991; and two in the long jump, in 1983 and 1987. He also won the Sullivan Award for Outstanding Amateur Athlete of the Year in 1981.

Lewis is in the top ten for most Olympic Medals won by men. He won two Gold Medals and one Silver at the 1988 Olympics; and two Gold Medals at the 1992 Olympics.

He also has a record seven World Championships. He won the Olympic 100 meters in 1984 and 1988, with times of 9.99 and 9.92, respectively. The 1988 mark was a world record at the time, which he himself bettered in 1991. Altogether, Lewis had 16 Gold Medals at the top level of sprint and long-jump competition at the close of 1993.

Lewis set an Olympic record in the 200 meters in 1984, with a time of 19.8 seconds. He won the long jump in 1984, 1988 and 1992, with leaps of 28 feet and one-quarter inch; 28 feet, seven and one-quarter inches; and 28 feet, five and one-half inches.

He also won Gold Medals for his part in the 400 meter Relay race in 1984 and 1992; as well as a Silver Medal in the 200 meters in 1988, coming in second to John DeLoach's then-Olympic record run of 19.75 for the distance. The 1992 Olympics Relay team set a World Record of 37.4.

There was speculation that 1993 was the beginning of the close of "The Lewis Era," when Lewis injured his back in an auto accident. Adding to that was his lack of wins in the 100 throughout 1993, plus an upset in the 100 by the UK's Linford Christie at the IAAF World Track and Field Championships in Stuttgart.

He is the only American to date to win the Tour de France, the world's greatest bicycle race, and he won it three times, in 1986, 1989 and 1990.

Gregory LeMond was born in Los Angeles on June 26, 1961, but the family moved to northwestern Nevada, where his father developed an avid interest in long-distance cycling. Greg became interested in cycling as his father took him along on his journeys.

In 1975, he joined the Reno, Nevada Wheelmen cycling club, and placed second in a 25-mile race in February 1976. In his first few months of competition, he won 11 races in his age group, then petitioned to be allowed to compete with 16 to 19-year-olds, and by year's end, had won the Nevada Junior championship, and placed fourth in the Nationals for Juniors.

From that time on, he devoted himself entirely to cycling, winning the Gold in the Junior Nationals in 1977, and a Bronze in the Junior World Championship Trials in 1978. In 1979, at the Junior World Championships in Buenos Aires, LeMond won a Gold, a Silver and a Bronze, becoming the first cyclist to win three medals in one world-class meet.

LeMond became the first American to win a major staged race when he won the European Circuit de la Sarthe race in April 1980. When the US boycotted the 1980 Olympics, LeMond went pro with the French Renault team. There, he fell under the coaching wisdom of the great Tour de France cyclist **Bernard Hinault (see no. 81)**.

He won the 1983 World Championship race, a dazzling 1.183 minutes faster than the runner-up, for a time of 7:1:21. Then, in 1984, despite a debilitating bout of bronchitis that held him to 15th place for two weeks of the race, he won an astonishing third place in the Tour de France — he was the first non-European to break into the top three.

In 1985, LeMond and Hinault were on a new team — La Vie Claire. Hinault came in first, LeMond second, in the Tour de France. The Tour de France of 1986 was historic. After an unexpected, all-out battle with Hinault, LeMond won the Tour de France for the first time, with a time of 110:35.19, which was three minutes and 19 seconds faster than Hinault.

His Tour Championship defense in 1987 was prevented by a broken wrist suffered in the spring of that year, and a near-lethal gunshot wound suffered during a hunting accident.

LeMond suffered a shin infection in 1988, and finally, in 1989, he was ready for the Tour again. He won it, proving his gritty strength and depth of talent. He then went on to win the World Championship, reasserting his status as the world's premier cyclist. He then signed a three-year, $5.5 million contract with the Z Team, also based in France. He won the Tour de France again in 1990.

Greg LeMond

She was the first gymnast ever to score a perfect 10 in Olympics competition. She did this as she won the Gold Medal in the Uneven Parallel Bars at the Olympics in Montreal, in 1976. Altogether, she won three Gold, two Silver and one Bronze medal in that Olympics. In 1980, she won two Gold and two Silver Medals.

Nadia Comaneci was born November 12, 1961, in Onesti, Romania. When she was six, she was taken under the wing of Bela Karoli, the great gymnastics teacher, while he was scouting public schools for potential members of the national junior gymnastics team.

In 1969, Nadia entered national competition, placing thirteenth. The next year, she won the Junior Championship. She then competed in and won numerous Eastern-bloc championships. Her first trip outside of the Communist sphere came in 1975, when she totally outclassed the competition at the European Championships at Skien, Norway. She walked away with four of the five Gold Medals.

Her style was uncannily precise, combined with a sense of balance in any position and a rock-like self-assurance that seemd to allow her to establish her own source of gravity. It seemed she could do anything, and she did.

In the qualifying meets for the 1976 Olympics, she scored six perfect scores out of eight. She then won the American Cup competition, earning several tens along the way. She was 15 years old, and the talk of the sports world.

In Montreal, she won Olympic Gold in

Nadia Comaneci

the All-Around; the Uneven Parallel Bars (with two perfect scores combined for 20 points) and the Balance Beam (with a near-perfect points total of 19.95); and she won a Bronze in the Floor Exercise.

She repeated her success in 1980, with Gold in the Balance Beam (19.8) and Gold in the Floor Exercise (tied with Nellie Kim at 19.875). She won a Silver Medal in the All-Around, which caused controversy, as her Romanian team felt she should have won the Gold. Bela Karoli accused the East German judge of lowering Comaneci's score.

Comaneci defected from Romania on November 1, 1989, arriving in New York City to become a citizen of the US, and to visit her former coach, Karoli, who was then residing in Texas.

Dubbed "The Great One" for reasons obvious to hockey fans, **Wayne Gretzky** is the most dominant hockey player in history. In addition to his blazing path of records, he also has influenced the way the game is played, with a brains-over-brawn style that de-emphasizes, but does not totally eliminate, the pugnaciousness for which hockey is known. He goes with a "check," not resisting it, but sliding around it, like a waiter in a crowded room.

He was born on January 26, 1961, in Brantford, Ontario. His dad had once played junior hockey, and Wayne was on skates as soon as he could walk. The ice rink in the back yard helped, too. His dad drilled him in all the essentials, and when Gretzky was six, he was competing against 10-year-olds.

He started playing professionally at the age of 17, with the Indianapolis Racers of the World Hockey League — the youngest athlete in North America to play on a major pro sporting team. After eight games, the Racers needed money and sold players to other teams. Wayne went to the Edmonton Oilers in the National Hockey League.

In his first eight years in the NHL, he won the Most Valuable Player eight years straight; he led the league in scoring for seven of those years; he was the playoffs MVP in 1985; and was awarded the Lady Byng Trophy for gentlemanly conduct in 1980.

In the season of 1981-82, he scored a staggering 92 goals and 120 assists. At six feet and under 180 pounds, he is not physically powerful, but he is deadly accurate with the puck, and he has incredible lateral speed on skates. He includes the upper corners of the goal in his target area, increasing the opportunity to score, and is a master stick handler, working wonders with the aspect of the blade. In 1988, he was traded by the Oilers to the Los Angeles Kings.

On March 23, 1994, Gretzky broke **Gordie Howe**'s **(see no. 45)** record for the most goals in an NHL career, when he made his goal number 802. It was his 1117th game in 15 seasons, versus the great Howe's career of 1767 in the NHL.

Gretzky currently holds or shares 63 NHL records, including all the major records. His career totals through March 1994 included 1646 assists, 2448 points, and 49 games in which he scored three or more goals. Single-season records he claims are: most goals in a season (92 in 1981-82); most assists (163 in 1985-86); most points (215 in 1985-86); and most consecutive games with a goal or an assist (51 in 1983-84). In the Stanley Cup playoff records, Gretzky has the most goals for a playoff career, 110; the most assists, 236; and the most points, 346.

Wayne Gretzky

94. FLORENCE GRIFFITH-JOYNER
b. 1962 (Track and Field Athlete)

She holds the World, Olympic and American records in the 100 and the 200 meter runs, at, respectively — 10.49 for the 100 meter; and 21.34 all for the 200 meter. She was also known for her unconventional one-legged running suits, designer running shoes and multicolored fingernails.

Having set school records in sprinting and the long jump at Los Angeles' Jordan High School, **Florence Delores Griffith** enrolled at California State University at Northridge, where she came under the tutelage of track coach Bob Kersee, who helped her technically.

She followed Kersee to UCLA, where she became NCAA Champion in the 200 meters run in 1982, with a time of 22.39 seconds. She won the NCAA 400 title, and was runner-up in the 200, in 1983. At the 1984 Olympics, in Los Angeles, she Silvered in the 200 behind long-time rival Valerie Brisco.

Griffith married Olympic Gold Medalist Al Joyner (brother of track star **Jackie Joyner Kersee [see no. 95]**, who was wife of Griffith's coach). In 1987, she won the 200 meters at the World Championship Games in Rome.

In the trials for the 1988 Olympics, she set a historic 100-meter record of 10.49, a full quarter-second off the previous record. No one in recorded history had beaten an existing 100 record by more than one-tenth of a second to that point. This occurred on July 16, 1988. Her previous run had been a 10.60, also a record-breaker, but officials ruled that she had been aided by the wind, and disallowed that mark. On July 17, she ran 10.70 and 10.61 — and became the first woman to run the four fastest times for the 100 in two consecutive days. She then set a US record for the 200, at 21.77, but shortly after the Olympic trials, she fired Kersee as her coach, deciding that her husband would serve in that capacity.

In the 1988 Olympics in Seoul, she set an Olympic record in winning the 100 at 10.54; and in the 200, at 21.34. She won a third Gold Medal in the 400-meter Relay race, and a Silver in the 1600-meter Relay.

She was named Sportswoman of the Year in France; and Athlete of the Year by the Soviet news agency TASS. In 1989, she won the US Olympic Committee Award, Berlin's Golden Camera Award; the Sullivan Award as the Top American amateur athlete; the Jesse Owens Award as the outstanding track and field athlete of the year; and the Harvard Foundation Award for outstanding contributions to society.

On February 25, 1989, she announced her retirement from competition, to tend to her far-flung and highly successful enterprises, which include fashion design, writing, acting, motivational speechmaking and being a media celebrity.

Florence Griffith-Joyner

95. JACKIE JOYNER-KERSEE
b. 1962 (Track and Field Athlete)

She has brought public attention and interest to the heptathlon with her marvellous ability. She holds the record in the heptathlon, with 7291 points scored at the 1988 Olympics, for the Gold. She also includes among her awards the Gold Medal in the 1988 Olympic long jump; the Gold in the 1992 Heptathlon; the Silver in the Heptathlon in the 1984 Olympics and the Bronze in the Long Jump in 1992.

Jacqueline Joyner was born in East St. Louis, Illinois, on March 3, 1962. When she was 12, she could broad jump more than 17 feet. Jackie took up the five-event pentathlon in her early teens, winning four consecutive National Junior Pentathlons. She then went to UCLA on a basketball scholarship, where she met track and field coach Bob Kersee, who became her coach, and eventually, her husband (on January 11, 1986).

In 1984, she missed the Gold Medal in the Olympics by .06 seconds in the final

event, due to a leg injury. In 1985, she set an American record in the Long Jump of 23 feet, nine inches. She was ranked third in the world. She set high points totals in college meets in 1986, scoring 6910 points at one and 6841 at another. No one had ever scored 7000 points.

Joyner-Kersee scored 7148 points at the Goodwill Games in Moscow that year, shattering the World Record by 200 points and breaking the 7000 barrier. She set an American record of 12.85 in the 100-meter hurdles, and a Heptathlon record of 23 feet in the Long Jump.

Less than a month later, at the US Olympic Festival in Houston, she broke her own record with 7161 points. She broke her American Long Jump record, too. Her *average* score in 1986 was in excess of 7000 points, putting her leagues above the competition.

She won the overall points championship at the Mobil Grand Prix Track and Field competition in 1987. She unofficially broke the American Women's 100-meter hurdles record at the Pepsi Invitational at UCLA; at the 1987 Pan-American Games, she equalled the world record in the Long Jump. At the Track and Field World Championships in Rome, she won Gold Medals in the Heptathlon (with 7128 points) and the Long Jump (24 feet, one and three-quarters inches). She was hailed as "America's Greatest Athlete Since **Jim Thorpe**" **(see no. 18).**

She has gone on to win in the Track and Field World Championships again, in 1991, with a long jump of 24 feet, one-quarter inch, and in 1993, with 6837 points in the Heptathlon. She won the Gold in the Olympics Heptathlon in 1992, and the Bronze in the Long Jump. In 1993, she won the World Track and Field Championships Heptathlon Gold Medal, with a score of 6837 points.

Jackie Joyner-Kersee

96. MICHAEL JORDAN
b. 1963 (Basketball Player)

Michael Jordan

The man who many regard as history's greatest basketball player, **Michael Jordan**, was born on February 17, 1963 in Brooklyn, New York. His mother and father showered him and his four brothers and sisters with love, devotion to the work ethic and common-sense understanding of avoiding delinquency and drugs.

Michael worked hard to develop his considerable abilities. In high school, he grew from five feet eleven inches to six feet, six inches tall. That was the deciding factor in his choice of basketball as a career. He went on to attend the University of North Carolina at Chapel Hill, earning an Atlantic Coast Conference Rookie of the Year Award for his peformance in Chapel Hill's NCAA Basketball Championship win over Georgetown.

Jordan was a unanimous All-American pick in 1982-83, and was the *Sporting News* College Player of the Year in 1983. He was an inspired player at guarding, shot-blocking, scoring, play-making, and stealing the ball. He could seemingly defy gravity with his soaring leaps.

He led Chapel Hill to the Atlantic Coast Conference regular season championship. Once again, he was named the *Sporting News* College Player of the Year.

That same year, the Chicago Bulls offered Jordan a five-year contract at seven figures, and he accepted. His first year, he led the NBA with 2313 points, became Rookie of the Year, was a starter in the All-Star Game, and was named Best Player in the NBA.

He missed most of the next season with a foot injury, but returned in time to pull the Bulls out of a slump that had cost them 43 of 64 games. With him, they made the playoffs, albeit losing to the Celtics — but not before Jordan scored 63 points in that single game, a record for most points in an NBA playoff game.

On April 16, 1987, he scored 61 points against the Atlanta Hawks, to push his total over 3000 that season, becoming only the second player in the history of the game to do so. He also scored a record 23 consecutive points in that game.

As of the end of the 1992-93 season he is credited with the following records, awards and accomplishments: most points in a playoff game, 63; regular season average, 32.3; All-Defense Team five consecutive times; All-Star Team six consecutive times; Playoffs MVP in 1991, 1992 and 1993; league leader in scoring seven consecutive seasons; led league in steals, three times; and Most Valuable Player in 1988, 1991 and 1992. He had also played on the 1984 USA Olympic basketball team and with **Magic Johnson (see no. 88)** on the USA 1992 Olympic "Dream Team," both of which won the Gold Medal in basketball.

A strange twist to the life of this affable, well-liked superstar was the shocking murder of his father by two young strangers in 1993. This event caused his retirement from basketball in 1993, at the peak of the most fabulous career in basketball history.

Also in 1993, he made the amazing switch from basketball to baseball. He signed a contract with the Chicago White Sox and they sent him to their Birmingham Alabama farm team.

97. MATTI NYKANEN
b. 1963 (Ski Jumper)

The most dominant ski jumper of the modern era, **Matti Nykanen** was born on September 17, 1963, in Finland. His native country's long winter and soaring mountainsides would be ideal for a boy growing up with ambitions of being a ski jumper.

A four-time Olympic Gold Medalist, he won the 90-meter jump in 1984 and 1988, and the 70-meter jump in 1988. He was the first man to win both events in one Olympics, and was the first Olympic champion to repeat in the ski jump since 1936, as well as being on the first Men's team to win the gold for the newly established team jumping competition.

He won the 1984 90-meter with 231.2 points, over Jens Weissflog, of East Germany. Weissflog beat him in the 70-meter, and Nykanen had to settle for the Silver Medal. He was also World Champion in the 90-meter in 1982, and has won four World Cups in jumping, in 1983, 1985, 1986 and 1988.

In 1988, in the Winter Olympics at Calgary, Nykanen won the Gold for the 90-meter jump with 224 points, and won the Gold for the 70-meter jump with 229.1 points. He won a third Gold for the newly-approved team jumping competition. He won the most Gold Medals of any man competing in that particular Winter Olympics.

In counterpoint to Nykanen's achievements as a jumper in Calgary, were the endearing attempts made by comedic, but apparently seriously-intentioned, Michael "Eddie the Eagle" Edwards, the sole jumping entrant from Great Britain. Edwards finished 58th and 55th in the 70-meter and the 90-meter jump, respectively.

Matti Nykanen

This Swiss alpine skier was a four-time World Cup Overall Champion, in 1984, 1987, 1988 and 1990. He was also a three-time runner-up for the honor. He won 40 World Cup events in 10 years, and also won one Gold and one Bronze Medal at the 1988 Olympics.

In 1987, **Pirmin Zurbriggen** dominated the world of Men's Alpine skiing, winning the World Cup Championship in the Giant Slalom, Super Giant Slalom, Downhill and Overall awards. His win of those four championships matched the great Jean-Claude Killy's four-title win in 1967.

In the 1988 Olympics, in Calgary, Zurbriggen was favored to win five Gold Medals. Two of the events would be contested for the first time. These were the Combined (one downhill run and two slaloms) and the "Super G," or Super Giant Slalom.

He won the Gold in the Downhill, but took a fall in the Slalom portion of the men's Combined, which Italian Alberto Tomba then won. Tomba also won the Giant Slalom. In March of that year, the tables were turned, when Zurbriggen clinched the World Cup Overall Men's Championship with a win over Tomba in the season's last Slalom race at Saalbach, Austria.

In 1990, Zurbriggen clinched his final, record-tying fourth World Cup Overall Championship with a win in a Slalom event in Veysonnaz, Switzerland. Zurbriggen announced that he would retire at the end of that season.

Pirmin Zurbriggen

She is the best wo-man speed skater ever to skate for the United States. In the Olympic Games at Lillehammer, in February of 1994, US Speed Skater **Bonnie Blair** won the 500-meter race (in 39.25) and the 1000-meter race (in 1:19.74), giving her an Olympics career total of five Gold Medals — the most Golds for any American wo-man Olympian. With a total of six medals overall (including a Bronze), she surpassed **Eric Heiden**'s (**see no. 86**) Winter Olympic medal record of five medals, giving her the most medals for any American Winter Olym-pian. She was also the first woman in any sport, or from any na-tion to win consecutive Olympic Gold Medals in the 500-meter race.

Bonnie Blair

She was born on March 18, 1964, in Cornwall, New York, one of many children in a large, happy family. The Blairs loved skating, especially competing at local meets. The family moved two years later to Champaign, Illinois, a hub of the US speed skating sport. Four of Bonnie's siblings grew up to become national champions.

Bonnie was winning races against nine and 10-year-old girls when she was just six years old. At seven, she competed in the state Championships. In 1979, she linked up with Olympic medalist and speed skat-ing coach Cathy Faminow, who encouraged Blair to work on her skating year-round. With fund-raising help from the Cham-paign Police Department, she set out to compete on the European circuit, and went to her first Olympics in 1984. She came away awed, but medalless, and determined to learn more — and the rest is history!

In 1988, she had won the Olympic Gold in the 500 and the Bronze in the 1000. She won the Gold in both events in the 1992 Olympics. That same year, Blair received the Sullivan Award for the outstanding am-ateur athlete of the year. In 1989, she was the World Sprint Champion.

She has been called the best technician in the world in the 500 and the 1000-meter races. Small for a speed skater, at five feet, four inches tall and 130 pounds, she has mastered her technique and gets everything possible out of each stroke of skate blade on ice.

100. KRISTEN OTTO
b. 1966 (Swimmer)

She is the first woman to win six Gold Medals at an Olympics. Four of the medals were for individual events, and two were for team events. She won a Gold Medal for each event she entered that year, and is in the Top Five of women having the most Gold Medals in the Summer Olympics.

Kristen Otto was born in 1966 in East Germany, when the then infamous "Wall" divided east from west. Shortly after her Olympic record, the Berlin Wall came down, and the "two Germanys," in existence since the end of World War II, were reunited into one country. In the resulting change, the East German swim team, of which Kristen Otto was a member, was integrated into that of West Germany to become the German national team.

Otto achieved her record with the East German team at the 1988 Olympic Games in Seoul. Afterward, she narrowly missed being chosen Top Athlete of 1988 by a poll of 36 nations conducted by the Soviet News Agency, TASS. Unfortunately for her, the poll chose **Florence Griffith Joyner (see no. 87)** over her. Otto finished second in the poll, and German tennis player Steffi Graf finished third.

Otto's six Golds were in the 50-meter Freestyle; the 100-meter Freestyle; the 100-meter Backstroke; the 100-meter Butterfly; the 4x100-meter Freestyle Relay; and the 4x100-meter Medley Relay.

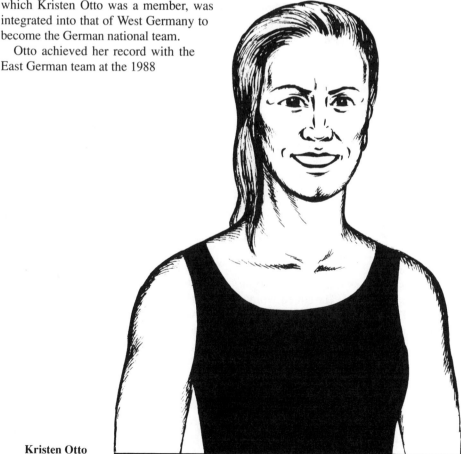

Kristen Otto

TRIVIA QUIZ & GAMES

1. This heavyweight from Manassa was once accused of doing something to his hands before a fight. Who was he, and what is he accused of? Had he done it, would it have worked? (see no. 22)

2. Thomas Topham was one of the great strong men of all time. But he had a lighter side, too. What object did he once displace to a new location? What was inside of it? (see no. 9)

3. A master base stealer, the "Georgia Peach" established a reputation for himself as a terror of the basepaths. What base did he steal fairly often, that is seldom stolen in this era? Who was the Georgia Peach? Was he always as "nice as a peach"? (see no. 17)

4. They were both players of a genteel sport. One was young and the other stood on the greens of age and wisdom. One of them cured the other's bad temper with a pithy answer. Who were they? What was the answer? What *was* the question it answered? Was their logic full of holes? (see no. 12)

5. What sport did Eric Heiden take up upon retirement from the sport that made him famous? What was the sport that made him famous? Has he ever been surpassed in any of his accomplishments? In the same sport? If so, by whom? (see nos. 86 and 99)

6. Red Grange was one of the all-time great ball carriers. He hailed from a small Pennsylvania town. What was the name of that town? How did he cause a controversy? What area of sport benefitted directly from his action? In how many ways? (see no. 27)

7. Her name was synonymous with figure skating, and she popularized it as no one has done before or since. Darryl F. Zanuch captured her in motion. Who was she? (see no. 30)

8. Bernard Hinault practically owned the Tour de France in his time. He was a Frenchman's Frenchman, and a national hero for his skills on a bicycle. Yet he was also tutor to an upstart who would not only prevent him from recording an insurmountable sixth win in the Tour de France, but would also challenge European cycling supremacy. Who was his pupil? Ironically, who did he ride for? (see no. 92)

9. "Barriers are made to be broken." Who said that? What specific barriers did he himself break? Which was the biggest one? (see no. 52)

10. The sound barrier was a challenge to jet pilots of the early 1950s. What was the equivalent barrier for runners? Who broke it? Who almost beat him to it, and why didn't he? (see no. 48)

11. Known for elegance and being a sparkling ambassador for his sometimes-maligned sport, he was only "behind the eight ball" every so often, in a strictly literal sense — and then not for long. Who was he? (see no. 33)

12. Jack Nicklaus has been called the greatest golfer ever. He even designs golf courses. What is his outstanding mental characteristic? What activity — teeing off, driving down the fairway, etc. — does he excel at? With all his interests as a very public representative of a lucrative sport, what comes first in his life for him? (see no. 60)

13. At first, she had an unhappy childhood, but a stepdad made all the difference. Another thing that made a difference were all the championships she won. In fact, she dominated Wimbledon as no other woman has done. What is the name of this fairly new citizen of the US (and when did she gain citizenship)? (see no. 84)

14. Her one-inch, multi-colored nails and the clothes she wore on the track created a sensation. Even more sensational, she set a record that was a full one-quarter of a second under the existing record. Who was she? What sport was she involved in? Is she still active? (see no. 87)

15. Even the Pope was excited to meet him, regardless of the fact that for most of the world, he was a man with just one single name — a name not even he knew the origins of. Name the man and his sport. Was he an ambassador for his sport? How? (see no. 62)

16. He was at first a miracle man in the Olympics, and suddenly, he was stripped of his medals. Even so, Jim Thorpe is still referred to as "America's Greatest Athlete." Thinking strictly in terms of its present name, what athletic assocation did he head as its very first president? (see no. 18)

17. Cassius Clay was his original name, but he changed it. He first lost his title in a KO by the courts. Why did he change his name and what was his new name? Why did he lose that first title? How many times did he win the title back? (see no. 64)

SUGGESTED PROJECTS

1. It has often been postulated that modern athletes enjoy distinct advantages over those who have gone before, by reason of advanced equipment, better playing fields, better diets, more systematic training regimens, etc. One theory even applies a handicap system based on the notion that the present, with a greater population than the past, should produce a greater number of top-level athletes.

An experiment was once conducted in which famous boxers statistics, styles, preferences and tendencies were fed into a computer for a series of computerized matches to see who the best boxer of all time was.

Assemble all the data you can find on each, and, taking into comparison such variables as equipment, number of matches played and number of opponents played — ie, intensity of competition — and rules changes, conduct your own survey to discern who the greatest woman tennis player of all time is. Then try it with the men.

2. Every sport requires mental, as well as physical ability. In fact, many top athletes also excelled academically, due to their will to perform well.

Do an informal comparison of various sports based on these characteristics: ie, tennis oviously requires strength, agility and a good tactical sense; by comparison, a race car driver sheds 10-15 pounds of weight in a 500-miler — what kind of physical and mental ability is required here — and would it be more or less intensive than playing Wimbledon?

Likewise, come-from-behind finishes are known in every sport. Is a come-from-behind harder in a sport where the only equipment is the athlete's own body, or is it harder in a sport in which equipment makes a big difference — as in yacht racing?

Under what conditions does the *will* to win prevail, if all other factors are equal?

INDEX